W9-AVD-049

CliffsNotes™
Delivering a Winning Job Interview

By Mercedes Bailey

IN THIS BOOK

- Get over your nervousness by being prepared
- Know which questions to expect and how to answer them
- Deliver a job interview that wins you an offer
- Reinforce what you learn with CliffsNotes Review
- Find more information about job interviews in CliffsNotes Resource Center and online at www.cliffsnotes.com

IDG Books Worldwide, Inc.
An International Data Group Company
Foster City, CA • Chicago, IL • Indianapolis, IN • New York, NY

About the Author

Mercedes Bailey has written numerous articles and books including various texts on economics for educational publishers as well as other financial topics. She is the President of Word Management, a firm that writes and edits print and multimedia materials for a variety of clients.

Publisher's Acknowledgments

Editorial

Project Editor: Colleen Totz

Associate Acquisitions Editor: Karen Hansen

Copy Editor: Tamara S. Castleman

Technical Editor: Arlene Hirsch

Production

Indexer: York Production Services, Inc.

Proofreader: York Production Services, Inc.

IDG Books Indianapolis Production Department

CliffsNotes™ Delivering a Winning Job Interview
Published by
IDG Books Worldwide, Inc.
An International Data Group Company
919 E. Hillsdale Blvd.
Suite 400
Foster City, CA 94404
www.idgbooks.com (IDG Books Worldwide Web site)
www.cliffsnotes.com (CliffsNotes Web site)

Library of Congress Catalog Card No.: 99-67165
ISBN: 0-7645-8548-7
Printed in the United States of America
10 9 8 7 6 5 4 3 2 1
1O/RT/RS/ZZ/IN

Distributed in the United States by IDG Books Worldwide, Inc.
Distributed by CDG Books Canada Inc. for Canada; by Transworld Publishers Limited in the United Kingdom; by IDG Norge Books for Norway; by IDG Sweden Books for Sweden; by IDG Books Australia Publishing Corporation Pty. Ltd. for Australia and New Zealand; by TransQuest Publishers Pte Ltd. for Singapore, Malaysia, Thailand, Indonesia, and Hong Kong; by Gotop Information Inc. for Taiwan; by ICG Muse, Inc. for Japan; by Intersoft for South Africa; by Eyrolles for France; by International Thomson Publishing for Germany, Austria and Switzerland; by Distribuidora Cuspide for Argentina; by LR International for Brazil; by Galileo Libros for Chile; by Ediciones ZETA S.C.R. Ltda. for Peru; by WS Computer Publishing Corporation, Inc., for the Philippines; by Contemporanea de Ediciones for Venezuela; by Express Computer Distributors for the Caribbean and West Indies; by Micronesia Media Distributor, Inc. for Micronesia; by Chips Computadoras S.A. de C.V. for Mexico; by Editorial Norma de Panama S.A. for Panama; by American Bookshops for Finland.
For general information on IDG Books Worldwide's books in the U.S., please call our Consumer Customer Service department at **800-762-2974.** For reseller information, including discounts and premium sales, please call our Reseller Customer Service department at **800-434-3422.**
For information on where to purchase IDG Books Worldwide's books outside the U.S., please contact our International Sales department at 317-596-5530 or fax **317-596-5692.**
For consumer information on foreign language translations, please contact our Customer Service department at **1-800-434-3422,** fax 317-596-5692, or e-mail rights@idgbooks.com.
For information on licensing foreign or domestic rights, please phone +1-650-655-3109.
For sales inquiries and special prices for bulk quantities, please contact our Sales department at 650-655-3200 or write to the address above.
For information on using IDG Books Worldwide's books in the classroom or for ordering examination copies, please contact our Educational Sales department at **800-434-2086** or fax **317-596-5499.**
For press review copies, author interviews, or other publicity information, please contact our Public Relations department at **650-655-3000** or fax **650-655-3299.**
For authorization to photocopy items for corporate, personal, or educational use, please contact Copyright Clearance Center, 222 Rosewood Drive, Danvers, MA 01923, or fax **978-750-4470.**

Table of Contents

Introduction 1
Why Do You Need This Book? 1
How to Use This Book 2
Don't Miss Our Web Site 3

Chapter 1: Scheduling the Interview 5
Preparing for the Call 5
A checklist for success 6
Using preparation time 7
Getting the Call 8
Listen to yourself 8
Phone etiquette 10
Networking over the phone 12
Making Arrangements 14
People to know 14
Places to go 15

Chapter 2: Doing Your Homework 16
Learning about the Company 16
Printed materials 19
People contacts 20
Learning about the Industry 22
Printed industry sources 22
Internet sources 23

Chapter 3: Practicing Your Interviewing Skills 24
Taking Inventory of Your Strengths and Weaknesses 24
Naming the things you do best 25
Naming your weaknesses 27
Knowing Which Questions You Can Expect .29
Tell me about yourself 29
Why do you want to leave (or why did you leave) your present job? 30
What are your career goals? 31
What contribution can you make to the company? 32
Getting Practice before the Interview 32
Role-playing an interview 33
Videotaping a practice interview 33

Chapter 4: Dealing with the Jitters **35**
  Confidence-Building: The RAPP Approach 36
    R is for research 36
    A is for appearance 37
    P is for preparation 38
    P is for practice, practice 39
  You're On: Five Tips for Dealing with Stage Fright 39
    Tip #1: Take a deep breath 40
    Tip #2: Smile 40
    Tip #3: Stretch 41
    Tip #4: Recognize the power of affirmations 41
    Tip #5: Stay in touch 42
  Being Realistic 42
    Making a good impression 43
    Getting additional information 44
    Getting a call back for a second interview 44
    Getting feedback 45

**Chapter 5: Mastering the Interview: Communicating Clearly
and Persuasively** **47**
  Strategies for Beginning the Interview 48
    Surviving small talk situations 48
    Transitioning to the main part of the interview 49
  Strategies for Questions and Answers 50
    Choose your words carefully 50
    Be honest 51
  Common Interview Questions 52
    Previous experience 52
    How others perceive you 53
    Why should we hire you? 54
    Salary expectations 56
    Past achievements 56
    Do you have any questions? 57

Chapter 6: Active Listening **58**
  Tip #1: Pay Attention 58
  Tip #2: Summarize What the Speaker Has Said 59
  Tip #3: Take Notes 60
  Tip #4: Ask for Feedback 61
  Tip #5: Practice Makes Perfect 62

Chapter 7: Handling Difficult Questions and Scenarios . . . . . . **.63**
Illegal or Inappropriate Questions 64
Questions about race, religion, or ethnicity 64
Questions about marital status and children 65
Questions about age, weight, health, or disabilities 66
Guidelines for handling illegal or inappropriate questions 67
Dealing with the Difficult Questions 68
Have you ever been fired? For what reasons? .68
Questions about being out of work 69
Questions about sexual harassment 70
Handling Difficult Scenarios 71
Panel interviews 71
Behavioral interviews 72
Situational interviews 73

Chapter 8: Closing the Interview . . . . **.75**
Recognizing the End of the Interview 75
Closing statements made by the interviewer .76
Non-verbal clues 76
Do you have any questions for me? 77
Speaking Your Last Words 78
Strategies for Lasting Impressions 80
One last impression on the interviewer 81
Out the door 81

Chapter 9: Getting the Second Interview . . . . **.83**
Appropriate Responses to the First Interview 83
Expressing your gratitude 84
Informing your networking contacts 87
Alerting your references 88
Second Interviews 89
The serial interview 89
The meal interview 90

Chapter 10: Negotiating Skills in the Interview Process . . . . . . **.93**
Learning What You're Worth 94
Sources of information 94
Experience is a good teacher 95
Timing the Salary Question 96
Strategies for delaying the discussion of salary 96
The timing is right: You've been offered the job 98

Five Tips for Negotiating Salary and Benefits 98
   Tip #1: Give yourself confidence and enthusiasm 99
   Tip #2: Let them make the first offer 99
   Tip #3: Enhance your compensation package 100
   Tip #4: Give yourself time 100
   Tip #5: Get it in writing 102

Chapter 11: Following Up **103**
   Composing Letters of Acceptance or Rejection 103
   What to look for in a written job offer 103
   Sample acceptance letter 105
   Writing a Letter of Resignation 107
   Before your resign 107
   Sample letter of resignation 109
   Networking Follow-up 110
   Making phone calls 110
   Sending your thank-yous 111

CLIFFSNOTES REVIEW **112**
   Q & A 112
   Scenario 114
   Consider This 114
   Practice Projects 114

CLIFFSNOTES RESOURCE CENTER **115**
   Books 115
   Internet 117
   Magazines & Other Media 118
   Send Us Your Favorite Tips 118

Index **119**

INTRODUCTION

Most people change careers several times in their professional lives. And within careers, people change jobs. Sooner or later, everyone needs solid interviewing skills. And tune-ups for these interviewing skills need to take place each time an occasion to use them occurs. CliffsNotes *Delivering a Winning Job Interview* provides just what you need to tune up your interviewing skills or introduce you to the world of interviewing for your first job.

CliffsNotes *Delivering a Winning Job Interview* is organized to help you from start to finish. The start happens before you walk into the interviewer's office. You start the interviewing process with solid preparation and practice. The process does not end when you walk out the interviewer's door, either. Only when you successfully conclude the process with a solid, acceptable job offer do you begin to conclude the interview.

Why Do You Need This Book?

Can you answer yes to any of these questions?

- Do you need to learn about job interviewing skills fast?

- Do you not have time to read 500 pages on delivering winning job interviews?

- Do you want to learn how to negotiate the best compensation for your next job?

- Do you need help in dealing with the jitters you feel before every job interview?

- Do you need practice in answering the most common questions asked in an interview?

If so, then CliffsNotes *Delivering a Winning Job Interview* is for you!

How to Use This Book

You're the boss here. You get to decide how to read this book. You can read the book from cover to cover or just look for the information you want and put it back on the shelf for later. However, I'll tell you about a few ways I recommend to search for your topics.

- Use the index in the back of the book to find what you're looking for.

- Flip through the book, looking for your topic in the running heads.

- Look for your topic in the Table of Contents in the front of the book.

- Look at the In This Chapter list at the beginning of each chapter.

- Look for additional information in the Resource Center or test your knowledge in the Review section.

- Flip through the book until you find what you're looking for — I organized the book in a logical, task-oriented way.

- Use the forms, checklists, and samples shown in the figures in most chapters to get the practice and skills you need for successful job interviewing.

Also, to find important information quickly, you can look for icons strategically placed in the text. Here are descriptions of the icons you'll find in this book:

If you see a Remember icon, make a mental note of this text — it's worth keeping in mind.

If you see a Tip icon, you know that you've run across a helpful hint, uncovered a secret, or received good advice.

The Warning icon alerts you to something that could be dangerous, requires special caution, or should be avoided.

Don't Miss Our Web Site

Keep up with the latest information about job interviews by visiting the CliffsNotes Web site at www.cliffsnotes.com. Here's what you find:

■ Interactive tools that are fun and informative

■ Links to interesting Web sites

■ Additional resources to help you continue your learning

At www.cliffsnotes.com, you can even register for a new feature called *CliffsNotes Daily*, which offers you newsletters on a variety of topics, delivered right to your e-mail inbox each business day.

If you haven't yet discovered the Internet and are wondering how to get online, pick up *Getting on the Internet,* new from CliffsNotes. You'll learn just what you need to make your online connection quickly and easily. See you at www.cliffsnotes.com!

CHAPTER 1
SCHEDULING THE INTERVIEW

IN THIS CHAPTER

- Getting the interview
- Making a favorable impression on the interviewer
- Attending to the details of setting up an interview appointment

Before you go on your winning job interview, you have to prepare for it. Winning interviews do not just happen. They are the result of careful planning, attention to detail, and research. The chapters that follow show you practical strategies for learning about the company, practicing interviewing skills, handling anxiety, developing better communication skills, handling difficult questions, and negotiating salary and other issues.

In this chapter, you make a checklist to identify all the things you need to do to prepare for that phone call that invites you to interview with the company of your dreams.

Preparing for the Call

Okay, you have sent your résumé with the best cover letter you could compose. Now what? Do you just sit by the phone hoping for the phone call to set up an interview? *No.* This is the time for tilling the field, laying the foundation, and making things happen. And here are some suggestions for turning the waiting period into the preparation period.

A checklist for success

You should use the time between sending your résumé and going to the interview as productively as possible. What you do in this in-between time can make the difference between success and failure in landing the job you want.

Take a look at the following checklist. You may think of other items to add to it because of the nature of your job search. Customize it to suit you own needs and situation. As you accomplish each item, cross it off your list. You gain energy and a sense of accomplishment as you take a proactive approach to getting that interview.

_____ 1. Learn about the company (see Chapter 2).

_____ 2. Use the Company Fact Sheet form to record contacts with the company (see Chapter 2).

_____ 3. Make networking calls to make contacts within the company.

_____ 4. Learn the exact location of the company.

_____ 5. Plan a travel route to the company to allow enough travel time.

_____ 6. Plan your wardrobe for the interview (see Chapter 4).

_____ 7. Organize forms, folders, or files for each company you contact.

_____ 8. Line up a friend or colleague to help you practice your interviewing skills (see Chapter 3).

_____ 9. Learn about salaries and job descriptions in the industry.

_____ 10.   Practice your telephone skills.

_____ 11.   Just in case you get a rejection or are ignored, make a list of 25 other companies that might be potential employers. Include names, addresses, phone numbers, and fax numbers for each.

_____ 12.   Other, please specify.

Using preparation time

After you send off your résumé and cover letter, you wait impatiently for a response. The days can lengthen into weeks, even months, without a phone call or letter from the company. Indeed, you may never hear from some companies that you sent your résumé to. Such companies may have been deluged with résumés. Or they may have advertised a position even though they already had someone in mind for the job before you even sent your résumé.

One of the first things you want to do as you prepare for the interview is develop a job-search calendar for yourself. Try the following steps:

1. Make or use a blank form for a month. You know the kind — seven squares across, five squares down. Label the month and add the appropriate number for the days of the weeks.

2. Invent a code or use abbreviations to identify each company you send a résumé to. Add a key to that code to the monthly calendar.

3. Consider using a color code for each company so that you can more easily track the chronology of your job search with each company.

4. Keep track of the important days of contact with the company. On the calendar, record the day you sent a résumé to the company, the day you get a phone call, the day(s) you make phone call(s), the day of the first interview, and so on.

5. Review this calendar every day and update it as necessary.

Getting the Call

Your job search is sure to involve calls that you make and calls that you receive. You will make calls to set up interviews and network with your professional contacts. You will receive calls from companies responding to your résumé. How you handle these calls may be just as important as the content and appearance of your résumé and your actual interviewing skills.

The following suggestions can help you improve your telephone skills and increase your chances of delivering a winning interview.

Listen to yourself

You may take your voice for granted, but for others, your voice is an important part of that important first impression. Consider how you sound to others. Try calling your own phone and listening to your answering machine or voice-mail message. How does it sound?

Is the quality of your voice pleasant? Is it energetic? Do you sound professional? What about the volume — do you speak too softly or too loudly? Have you done a grammar and slang check recently?

Try to listen to your own answering machine with the same objectivity a potential employer would have listening to you for the first time. This could be a good time to change your voice mail or answering machine message. Avoid slang, goofy music, or sound effects. Your aim is to project a friendly, professional tone and message.

Before you record a new message, write out what you want to say and practice saying it until it sounds natural and appropriate for your job search. You can use any of the following, or you can write your own.

OPTION A Hello. You have reached _____ (Name. Give the name you want the interviewer to use, not a "nickname"). I cannot take this call now but would like to contact you when I return. Please leave your name and phone number at the sound of the tone. If there is a convenient time for me to contact you, please leave that information as well. I am sorry to have missed you. Good-bye.

OPTION B Hello. You have reached the answering machine of _____ (Name. See Option A.) because I am unable to take this call at this time. I apologize for the inconvenience of leaving a message, but if you will leave your name and phone number, I will return this call as soon as possible. Please wait for the tone. Thank you for calling. Good-bye.

OPTION C Greetings. You have contacted the voice mail of _____ (Name. See Option A.). I am sorry to have missed your call. Please leave your name and phone number at the sound of the tone and I will return this call as soon as possible. Thank you for calling and I look forward to speaking with you soon. Good-bye.

Remember

Keep a résumé near your phone at all times so that you do not have to fumble around trying to find it after you get a call from a potential employer. Also keep your record sheet, calendar, and note paper close at hand. Make sure that your pen has ink in it.

Phone etiquette

The following are some basic do's and don'ts for the kind of phone skills and etiquette you want to develop for your successful job interview.

DO's

■ **Be prepared.** If you are initiating a call to get information about a name, correct spelling, directions, or a fax number, have your questions or script written out in front of you. Write the answers down as you get them.

■ **Be brief.** If you're calling to request information from a receptionist or from the human resources department, keep your questions simple and direct. This is not an opportunity to promote your own candidacy for the job.

■ **Speak clearly.** If you're nervous, write out a script and practice saying it before making the call. Speak slowly, distinctly, and in a friendly yet professional tone. On the phone, you can always refer to your notes or script.

■ **Call early.** People are often running to meetings or attending to their work during regular business hours. If you plan to call between 8:00 and 9:30 a.m., your chances of catching the person before a meeting are greater.

■ **Practice your voice-mail message before you make the call.** You will probably have to leave a voice-mail message sometime in the course of your job search. Playing "telephone tag" is not much fun. When you make a phone call, be prepared to leave a voice message. Write this out so that your name, number, and the reason for your call are clear and distinct. Even if you think the person has your telephone number, leave it on the voice mail as a courtesy. Leave times of availability to help prevent phone tag.

- **Be polite.** Remember your please and thank you. If you know the name of the person with whom you are speaking, refer to the person by name when thanking him or her or saying good-bye. Better to be more formal and use Mr. or Ms. than risk using a first name when doing so is not appropriate. Receptionists, assistants, and secretaries should be treated with respect even if you find their gatekeeping responsibilities aggravating.

- **Speak to the phone with a smile.** This might sound silly, but smiling while you talk on the phone conditions the tone of your voice and conveys a warmth and energy that is at least as important as what you actually say.

- **Follow up.** After you send a résumé or fax, a follow-up call to make sure that the communication has been received is often a good idea. Be brief, however. The follow-up call is not the time to try to set up an appointment.

DON'Ts

- **Don't call if the job posting indicates "no calls."** In this case, you could follow up sending your résumé after five days or a week with a note or fax asking for confirmation that the résumé has been received. If the job posting gives an e-mail address, sending your résumé and cover letter in this manner is fine. Always check to see that your material went through, however.

- **Don't use a false name.** When making your first calls to a company, never use a false name to acquire information or try to disguise your voice so that it won't be recognized if you call again. Never attempt to deceive a potential employer.

- **Don't be a pest.** Avoid unnecessary phone calls (like calling to verify the spelling of a name after you just asked that question in the previous phone call). Avoid too many requests to speak to your target person directly if the gatekeeper is screening calls.

- ■ **Don't seem disorganized or disinterested.** Organize your notes about previous conversations and communications so that you can be precise and to the point when you speak to your target person in the company. If suggestions are made to contact someone else or inquire about another position, do so. Then follow up with a note or another call thanking the person for the suggestion.

- ■ **Don't be timid.** You may experience some anxiety in making a cold call or contacting an unfamiliar person. Don't let your fears prevent you from making the calls you need to make to gain the interview. If you are prepared with a written script or written questions and practice your phone skills, you will conquer your anxiety.

Networking over the phone

Networking is the process of making and keeping business contacts to develop professional relationships based on sharing information and offering support and assistance.

Once you target a company, you can try to identify people inside the company who would be willing to talk with you about the company. The best way to do that is through networking. For example, you may ask your business friends, relatives, neighbors, or colleagues if they know anyone who knows, or might know, someone at your target company.

Once you identify someone who knows or might know someone at the company, ask if you can use his or her name when you make the call. Be sure to get the phone number from your networking source and repeat it after he or she gives it to you, to verify the number.

Prepare carefully for this kind of networking call. If you're calling a stranger who was referred to you, write down how you will introduce yourself. You might say something like this:

"Hello, I am ____ (name), a friend (colleague, relative, or whatever is appropriate) of ____ (name of person who referred you). ____ (name of referral) is helping me in my job search for ____ (name position). I have recently sent a résumé to _____ (name of company or person) in response to an advertisement (or job posting, or recommendation of a business colleague). _____ (referral's name) suggested that I contact you because you _____ (know the industry, know the company, know someone in the company, or whatever is appropriate) Do you have a few minutes to talk to me now, or may I call you back at a better time?

After that initial introduction, you should be prepared with several questions you want to ask. Write them down. They might include

- What educational or experience requirements would you look for in a candidate for the position I am hoping to get with (name of company)?

- What qualities do you think contribute most to success in this field?

- Do you have any advice for someone interested in this field?

- Do you know anyone at ____ (name of particular company) with whom I might talk to prepare myself for an interview?

- Do you know other people I could talk with who ____ (could help me learn more about the industry, could help me learn more about the company, might be helpful in my particular job search)?

Always follow up a networking call with a thank-you note to both the person who referred you and the person you talked with about the job, industry, company, and so on. If you know the person very well, this note may be handwritten, but generally, such notes are more professional and easier to read if they are typed.

Making Arrangements

Suppose that your résumé, preparations, and networking paid off and you got the call. You have been invited to an interview. Now you have people to know and places to go. Once again, the old scout motto, "Be prepared," is a strong ally.

People to know

Several people are involved in the interview process. Learn the name of the person who called you to set up the interview. Learn the name(s) of the person(s) who will interview you. Verify spellings of these names with the person making the call. At the same time, ask what their titles are within the company. You can do so by asking what department they are in and their positions.

Even if the name(s) seem common, double-check the spelling. For example, if you will be interviewed by Carol Smith, ask if that is Carole with an "e" and Smith or Smyth. Repeat the spelling after he or she gives it to you and record it on your Company Fact form (see Chapter 2).

Tell the person who made the call to set up the interview that you look forward to meeting him or her in person when you come in for the interview. Then make a point of greeting that person by name when you arrive.

Ask the person who calls you for the name and number of the person to call if you have further questions or need assistance prior to the interview. In most cases, the person to call is the person making the initial phone call.

Places to go

Even though you think you know the location of the company, ask the person calling you about the best way to get to the location. If you're planning to drive, ask if company parking is available. If appropriate, ask what floor the company occupies or on what floor you should meet the receptionist.

Once you have the proper information about the location of the company, figure out how much time to allow for travel. If you feel more comfortable and have the time, make a trial run to the company just so you know what to expect in terms of travel time and complications.

Always allow plenty of time to arrive at the interview. Give yourself an additional 15 to 30 minutes to travel so that you will not experience anxiety if you encounter some unforeseen delay.

Tip

Carry a cell phone and the company phone number with you, if possible, so that in the event of an unexpected and unavoidable delay, you can make a call while you are in transit to alert the interviewer of the problem.

Carefully record the date and time of the interview on your job-search calendar. Be there on time.

You still have things to do to get ready for the big interview. The following chapters give you suggestions about how to do your research, how to practice your interviewing skills *before* the big day, how to communicate clearly, listen carefully, and handle difficult questions or situations, and how to establish realistic goals for the interview.

CHAPTER 2

DOING YOUR HOMEWORK

IN THIS CHAPTER

- Learning about the company before the interview
- Keeping up-to-date about trends in the industry in which you are seeking employment
- Researching information in reports and on the Internet

Part of being prepared for your job interview is doing your homework so that you are knowledgeable about the industry and the company where you are seeking employment. For example, if you are interviewing with a hospital for an accounting position, you want to know something about the health care industry and the specific hospital.

A variety of ways are available to do the kind of research you need to answer and ask significant questions during your interview. This chapter examines how print materials, the Internet, and people can help you get the information you need for a winning interview.

Learning about the Company

One sure way to blow an interview is for you to lean back and say to the interviewer, "So tell me about what this company does." If the company is publicly held, you are expected to know something about the company, its products or services, and its annual revenues. If the company is privately held, you may not be able to get information about its revenues.

Take a look at the following Company Fact Sheet worksheet, which gives you an idea about the kind of information you should have before you go to the company for your interview. You may want to make a copy of this worksheet for each company to which you send a résumé. You can complete the basic information when you send out the résumé and research the rest when you have an interview lined up.

Company Name _____

_____

Address_____

_____

Phone/Fax Numbers _____

_____

Directions _____

_____

Contact Person _____

_____

Title _____

_____

E-mail _____

Networking Contact _____

Company Description _____

_____

Number of Employees _____

Number of Locations _____

Ownership _____

Names of Officers, Senior Management _____

_____

Annual Revenues _____

Major Competitors _____

Trends, Developments in Industry _____

Other Useful Information _____

Date(s) of Interviews _____

_____

Position Job Title _____

Job Description _____

_____

Salary Range _____

Reports to _____

Other Useful Information _____

_____

_____

To gather the information you want to make a great impression during your interview, you can use printed materials, the contacts you have, and, in some cases, the Internet.

The more you know about the company's products, profitability, markets, and activities, the greater the likelihood that you will appear to be a "good fit" for the job.

Printed materials

Many sources of printed materials are available that can give you valuable information about the companies that interest you. These include the annual reports that every publicly held company publishes, financial publications that provide current information about the status of companies, and directories that contain information about the names of company officers, sales, and products.

An annual report is produced every year and sent to the stockholders of a company. These reports usually contain a message from the chairman of the board as well as information about sales and performance. When you read an annual report, you learn something about the "personality" of the company and its current expectations. Most provide the company's mission statement that provides insight into the company's values.

You can get a copy of a company's annual report by calling the company and requesting a copy from the shareholder relations department. You also can get copies from the public library or through personal stockbrokers.

Financial publications are also a valuable source of information about a specific company. These are commonly available through stockbrokers, most of who are willing to send you a copy of a publication's evaluation of a company. Two popular financial publications are *The Value Line Investment Survey* and *S&P Investor's Kit*. Both of these publications offer special short-term subscription prices to individuals.

Various directories also contain a wealth of information about public as well as private companies. A few are listed here:

■ *Directory of Leading Private Companies.* Profiles 22,000 companies with sales of $10 million or more annually. Includes information about department managers.

■ *Million Dollar Directory Series.* Published by Dun and Bradstreet, this five-volume series provides information for more than 160,000 companies.

■ *Standard & Poor's Register of Corporations, Directors, and Executives.* These three volumes contain information about U.S. and Canadian companies, both public and private, including biographical data for 70,000 key executives.

These directories, and others, are available at your local library. In addition, local Chambers of Commerce usually publish directories that contain information about member companies. This information includes when the company was founded, the names of the key executives, and a description of its products or services. You can call the local Chamber of Commerce for a copy or visit your local library.

Joining your local Chamber of Commerce is often a good way to network with business people in your area. These contacts can be a valuable source of information.

People contacts

Networking with other business professionals has no substitute. Through your business contacts, you share information, swap tips, and expand the number of people you can access for information or assistance.

Networking is the process of making and keeping business contacts to develop professional relationships based on sharing information and offering support and assistance.

People who work inside a company know the place and business best. Your best source of information is often the employees who work there. One of your objectives in preparing for a winning interview is to get to know people inside the company before you go on your interview.

When you prepare for an interview, use your networking contact(s) to learn more about the company. If you know someone who knows someone who works for the company where you will be interviewed, ask for a referral. A referral occurs when the person you know gives you the name of somebody he or she knows within the company and gives you permission to contact that other person using his or her name as your entree.

Referrals are much better than "cold calls," when you must introduce yourself to a stranger hoping to obtain information. Based on the strength of the personal and professional network, the person you contact through a referral is much more likely to be friendly and helpful and take the time to answer your questions.

Before you contact a person in the company to get information for your interview, write down your questions so that you don't seem disorganized. Write down the answers as well. Also, double-check the spelling of the name of the person you are contacting so that you can write a thank-you note after your call.

In the course of your interview, you may find a way to let the interviewer know that you have been in contact with (name). You could say something like "I spoke with Ann Smith about her work here and was impressed with both the accomplishments and goals the company has set for itself."

Learning about the Industry

You need to know specific information about the particular company and its place in the entire industry. The trends, the economy, legislation, new developments, and technology all affect the entire industry. You want to appear knowledgeable and up-to-date about the latest trends and how they might affect the particular company.

Learning about an entire industry involves reading economic publications and could also include getting information off the Internet.

Printed industry sources

Business newspapers, national magazines and professional journals, and the entire news media offer many articles and data about every industry in this country and beyond. The volume of information can be overwhelming. Just stay focused and limit the amount of time and research you do.

For a basic overview of the major industries in the United States, consult the *U.S. Industrial Outlook.* This reference is published by the U.S. Department of Commerce and provides descriptions of 350 industries. You can learn about the major trends affecting each industry and the impact of foreign competition.

In addition, try consulting the *Career Guide to America's Top Industries,* published by the U. S. Department of Labor. This reference includes an overview of 40 major industries and identifies the types of jobs each offers, salary expectations, training required, advancement opportunities, and industry trends.

Every industry also has professional journals that publish articles about the latest developments and trends affecting it.

They also include profiles of some of the leaders in the industry. This information is especially helpful in your interview process.

National magazines and newspapers also provide useful information about a variety of industries.

Internet sources

The Internet contains more information than any individual can possibly assimilate. For example, if you want to get current information about the pharmaceutical industry from the Internet, simply connect to your server, type **"pharmaceutical industry"** (including the quotes), select your search engine, and ask it to identify the possible sources. This particular search yielded over 2.2 million Web sites connected to this topic. Many of the search engines rate the sources they identify and give the top-rated sites priority ranking.

After you find Web sites that offer you the most relevant information, you may want to bookmark these addresses and add them to your list of favorites for easy access.

Most pharmaceutical industries also advertise in popular magazines or news publications. These advertisements usually contain the company's Web site address. You can connect to these Web sites for additional useful information.

Learn to limit your time on the Internet; you cannot possibly check out everything you find. Save the more useful addresses in your favorites list to make future searches easier.

You need to learn a lot before you set out on your interview. Make use of your local library, the Internet, and above all, your personal contacts to impress your interviewers with your knowledge of the company and the industry.

CHAPTER 3
PRACTICING YOUR INTERVIEWING SKILLS

IN THIS CHAPTER

- Taking notes to prepare for questions and answers

- Anticipating questions about your past performance and future goals

- Getting practice before you go on the actual interview

Interviewing is like so many other skills — the more you do it, the better you get. Part of the difficulty is that nobody likes to have to think about participating in numerous interviews. Reaching the bulls-eye on the first try is *always* the hope, even if that hope is unrealistic. Even landing one job offer usually takes more than one interview. Doing it right is important.

In this chapter, you learn how to get practice for your winning interview without going into the situation cold. With practice, you can prepare yourself mentally and emotionally for your important interview. With this preparation, you gain confidence in your ability to handle difficult questions and present your experience in a positive light.

Taking Inventory of Your Strengths and Weaknesses

In almost every job interview, you will be asked some variation on the questions "What are your strengths?" and "What are your weaknesses?" You should come to an interview prepared with your responses.

Naming the things you do best

Consider the question, "What are your strengths?" to be a gift, an opportunity to present yourself in the best light. You do not want to boast or be overly modest. Be prepared to mention at least four or five strong points with examples that support each point you make.

For example, if you think that one of your strong points is your ability to work with numbers, you might support that with an example by saying, "I have good skills with numbers and was able to assist my manager with preparing the department budget in less time than it had taken him the year before."

Think of your strong points and skills in several different categories. Those categories could include

- **Intellect:** The ability to think quickly; to think logically; to express ideas clearly in writing, verbally, or artistically; to see the "big picture," problem solving; and creative thinking

- **Training/experience:** Education and job training; awards, certificates, and accomplishments; and volunteer experience

- **Personality/people skills:** The ability to handle conflict, leadership, teamwork, and enthusiasm

Ask a friend, mentor, or trusted colleague to help you identify your strengths and weaknesses on the job. You can learn a great deal from listening to others discuss their impressions.

Take the time to work on the following worksheet. If a question doesn't apply to you, skip it. If you think of other skills and strengths that do apply to you, mention them here.

Intellectual Skills   **Example**

1. Quick thinking _____

2. Detail oriented _____

3. Big-picture thinking _____

4. Best form of expression _____

5. Problem-solving _____

6. Other, name _____

Training/Experience   **Example**

1. Education _____

2. Certification _____

3. On-job training_____

4. Most effective job skill(s) _____

5. Recognition _____

6. Volunteer experience _____

7. Other, name _____

Personality/People Skills   **Example**

1. Strong personality traits_____

2. Leadership skills _____

3. Conflict-resolution skills _____

4. Teamwork skills_____

5. Management skills_____

6. Other, name _____

You may not have the opportunity to mention all the strengths you have identified, but you will feel more confident knowing that you have a repertoire to draw from. Tailoring your responses based on your understanding of the position, company, and industry can help you as well.

You can use job descriptions and networking information to find out which strengths are important, but you can also pick up clues to which strengths an interviewer values by the way a question is phrased. For example, if an interviewer asks about your people skills or asks for an example of teamwork, you realize that this is important to the company. Your Inventory of Strengths can help you provide the example(s) you need to have a winning interview.

Naming your weaknesses

There comes a time when you have to confront your limitations as well as your strengths. The interviewer may camouflage the weakness question in various ways. You might hear, "What would you like to improve about your job performance?" or " How have you grown professionally in the past three years?" These questions are designed to lead you to identify the areas that present the greatest challenge to you on the job.

Never take offense or become defensive at such questions. Instead, look at them as opportunities to turn lemons into lemonade. With practice, you can mention weaknesses that can easily be turned into strengths. For example, you might mention that you tend to give a lot of time to individual customers. That could be considered a weakness — if it implies that you do not give enough time to something else that is important. To turn that into lemonade, you can mention that while you give customers a lot of your time, they get better service as a result.

Think of three weaknesses you think you have. For each characteristic you identify, think of something practical you can do to overcome it. Then think of how you can turn this statement of weakness into something positive. Consider this example and then complete the following worksheet.

Weakness: I prefer to work independently rather than as part of a team.

Example/Proof: I will share a question I have about work and ask a colleague for a suggestion.

Lemonade statement: I am a self-starter and work quickly when I have a project to complete.

Weakness:_____

Example/Proof: _____

Lemonade Statement: _____

Weakness:_____

_____

Example/Proof: _____

Lemonade Statement: _____

Weakness:_____

Example/Proof: _____

Lemonade Statement: _____

Share this list of weaknesses with a trusted colleague or friend. This person may have good suggestions for correcting the weaknesses you have identified. Another strategy for dealing with weaknesses is to cite a learning goal, such as getting more computer training, and then working to achieve that goal.

Knowing Which Questions You Can Expect

Before you actually settle into the job interview, you'll probably be asked questions about the weather, the commute, and so on. This small talk may seem to you to be unimportant to the interview. These questions and comments are important, however, because they reveal a bit of your attitude and communication style to the interviewer.

Whatever the circumstances, always respond in a positive way. For example, if the interviewer asks if you had trouble finding the location or finding parking, simply say that you had no trouble. You might mention that you had asked the receptionist for directions, you had studied a map, or the cabdriver knew the route.

Once the small talk is over, you can expect to hear some of the following questions (in addition to questions about your strengths and weaknesses).

Tell me about yourself

To prepare for this question, jot down the highlights around these three points:

1. Your background (where you grew up, interesting or unusual or relevant facts about your family)

_____

_____

2. Your education and training (mention high school only if you are not a college graduate or if some experience there reveals a major strength or direction in your life)

_____

_____

3. Your work experience (mention recent experience, titles, job responsibilities, significant accomplishments)

_____

_____

Then come up with a transition statement — find a way to link your background and previous experience to your interest in the position you're being interviewed for. For example, "All of this brings me to my strong interest in the position you have available . . . ."

Practice your answer to this kind of interview question to limit your response to two or three minutes.

Why do you want to leave (or why did you leave) your present job?

Your response to this question is important, especially if you have been fired, downsized, or pressured to leave. No matter what your previous situation, never become defensive or speak negatively about your present/previous company or boss. If you're seeking another position as a path to career advancement, you also need to rehearse how you say so.

If you were fired from a previous job, you might say, "The truth is, I was fired. My boss and I had different management styles — she was more authoritarian and I am more collegial in working with colleagues." The interviewer may follow up by asking for an example. Be prepared to give a couple of examples. Practice describing your situation so that what another organization perceived as a weakness will seem like a strength in the company you are interviewing with.

If you were downsized, you might say, "The company was looking for ways to reduce expenses to enhance its bottom line. The entire technical department was let go. Unfortunately, I got caught in that."

If you were pressured to leave, you might say, "When I was transferred to customer service, I was not using my strengths and training in warehouse management, so I want to pursue a career more in line with my experience and training."

If you're interviewing for a position while you're currently employed, speak positively about your current situation and colleagues but emphasize your interest in career development and professional growth in a new situation.

What are your career goals?

The interviewer wants to assess your drive and aspirations and see how they fit with the company's goals. You want to prepare a response to this type of question so that you don't come across as arrogant or uncertain.

For example, you do not want to say that your goal is to become the Chief Technical Officer of the company within five years. But you could say something like, "Within the next two years, I hope I could advance to the level of Product Manager with the assistance of the present Director. Then I could be prepared to be promoted to Executive Director for the product line." Always indicate that your first goal is to learn to do your job well and make a significant contribution to the company's mission.

After you learn more about the industry and company you're interviewing with, practice describing your hoped-for career growth and advancement within the structure of the specific company.

What contribution can you make to the company?

Employers are always interested in how an employee can contribute to improved customer service, profitability, scheduling, or quality assurance. After you research the company, you can target one of its major points of emphasis and indicate how your skills and experience can impact the company positively. Have an example ready from your previous work experience that is comparable to what you've said you can do for the company you're interviewing with. (Chapter 7 addresses other questions you have to answer during the interview.)

Getting Practice before the Interview

The more prepared you are for an interview, the more confident you will be. A job interview is too important to leave to chance. A winning job interview is the result of hard work and practice on your part.

You can gain valuable interviewing experience in a couple of ways: You can prepare your responses to the questions you anticipate and then ask a friend or trusted colleague to role-play the interview process with you, or you can videotape one of your practice sessions.

Role-playing an interview

You're ready to ask someone to help you practice the inter-view process by role-playing after you do two things:

- Complete the worksheets in this chapter.

- Prepare a list of questions and answers you think you may have to deal with in an interview.

There may be interview questions that are specific to the industry or company you are approaching. Do not stop with the questions touched on in this chapter. Ask friends who have recently interviewed about the questions they were asked.

When you ask someone to role-play the interview process with you, make the setting of the role-playing as similar to the real office scene as possible. The person role-playing the interviewer should be at a desk. Ask that person to prepare a list of ten questions to ask you. You might give that person half the questions, but the interviewer should have some sur-prise questions for you to give you some practice in thinking on your feet.

Practice the introductory small talk as well as your conclud-ing remarks in your role-played interview.

After role-playing, go through a debriefing session. Ask the "interviewer" for feedback. Share with that person what you think went well and what you think you need to improve. If your friend is willing, ask if you can practice again after you work out more satisfactory responses for the practice interview.

Videotaping a practice interview

If you can, videotape one of your practice interview sessions. (If you think that the video camera will make you more nerv-ous, Chapter 4, on dealing with the jitters, may be helpful.)

Whether you're nervous or not, reviewing the video helps you become more objective about how you come across in an interview.

When you review a videotaped interview, look for things described in the following checklist and then work on correcting them. Evaluate yourself on a scale of 1 to 5 (5 being the best) on each of the following points. You might also ask others to view the videotaped practice interview and evaluate your interviewing skills.

_____ 1. Initial appearance

_____ 2. Body language (smile, handshake, posture, nervousness)

_____ 3. Handling initial introductions and small talk

_____ 4. Response to question(s) about strengths

_____ 5. Response to question(s) about weaknesses and failures

_____ 6. Response to question(s) about background

_____ 7. Response to question(s) about difficult situations

_____ 8. Response to question(s) about accomplishments

_____ 9. Response to question(s) about career goals

_____ 10. Response to close of interview

Things I want to improve: _____

_____

Practicing for your important job interview is the best strategy for having a winning interview.

CHAPTER 4

DEALING WITH THE JITTERS

IN THIS CHAPTER

- Facing that nervous feeling
- Building self-confidence for comfortable interviewing
- Setting realistic expectations for the first interview

Everyone feels nervous before an interview — that's normal. The interview process is important because a company uses it as a test — a test of your skills in communication and persuasion. Your ability to communicate what you know as well as persuade that you are the candidate best suited to the company's expectations is a formidable task.

One way to approach the interview experience is with the attitude that it is a win-win situation. You win if you eventually get the job you interview for — and you win valuable experience even if you don't get this particular job. With this attitude, you can build your confidence and deal with the customary nervousness knowing that something good will come out of the interview no matter what decision the company makes.

In this chapter, you learn the RAPP approach to building self-confidence for your winning interview as well as practical suggestions for dealing with the stage fright that you might experience as you wait for the actual interview. Finally, you learn to set some realistic expectations for your first interview with a company.

Confidence-Building: The RAPP Approach

The RAPP approach to building your confidence for your winning interview is based on many of the things presented in previous chapters. The four elements involved in the RAPP approach are the four cornerstones to the foundation for your self-confidence:

- **R** stands for the *research* and information you have about the company and the industry.

- **A** stands for your *appearance* as you go to the interview well groomed and confident about how you look.

- **P** stands for the *preparation* you have put into networking, getting directions, and learning names.

- **P** stands for the repeated *practice* you have given your interviewing skills.

R is for research

Your confidence stands on the research you have done about the company and the industry for which you are being interviewed. Review the completed Company Fact Sheet (see Chapter 2) the night before your interview. Bring the completed worksheet with you to the interview. You may have time to review it again as you wait for your interview.

When you took any test in the past, whether in college, applying for a driver's license, or qualifying for a sports competition, you remember that you felt more confident about taking the test when you had studied or prepared yourself in the appropriate way. The same is true for your winning job interview. The research or study you have done about the company gives you a sense of confidence.

A is for appearance

Your appearance when you present yourself at the interview is part of that all-important first impression. You don't get a second chance to make a good first impression. Take care that your appearance is not a matter of chance — but give it careful consideration.

Take a good look in a full-length mirror. Try to see yourself for the first time. Do not be overly critical or accepting of what you look like. Just be objective. When seeing you for the first time, what do you think a stranger notices?

Use the following checklist to help you take heed of your appearance and the impression you and your wardrobe can make on the interviewer. Rank yourself using a 5-point scale. Identify at least two things you will do to improve your appearance in each area.

1. Posture. "Stand up straight" was good advice from your parents and is good advice now. Practice walking toward the full-length mirror until you are comfortable with what you see. Pull a chair to the front of the mirror and practice sitting down and getting up from it. How do you look? Look closely at how you appear with your legs crossed.

Improvements

_____

_____

2. Grooming. Take a hard look at your hair. Do you need a new hairstyle, haircut, or hair color? You will make gestures with your hands. See your hands as the interviewer does. They need to be clean, with nails trimmed and shaped. Avoid gaudiness in ring(s) or other jewelry you wear. Avoid strong personal fragrances.

Improvements

_____

_____

_____ **3. Wardrobe.** Choose what you wear to the interview carefully. The old axiom "Dress for Success" holds true. Plan your wardrobe as if you already work in the position you are applying for. Your basic suit should be clean, pressed, and conservatively accessorized. Pay attention to your shoes. Are they polished, comfortable, and well heeled? Don't forget your hose. Are you color-coordinated?

Improvements

_____

_____

_____ **4. Accessories.** Consider the impression that your wristwatch, briefcase, tie, scarf, wallet, purse, and so on make when you first walk through the interviewer's door. This is not the time to wear your favorite Mickey Mouse watch. Keep things simple yet elegant.

Improvements

_____

_____

If you're in doubt about your appearance, ask a friend with the best taste to view your interview wardrobe and make suggestions.

P is for preparation

When you know where you're going, how long it will take you to get there, and the names and phone numbers of the people you will be talking to, you have no reason to feel the jitters because of being unprepared. You have prepared information about the company. Your Company Fact Sheet has been completed and reviewed. You have prepared your wardrobe and you feel confident about your appearance. You have attended to the details of directions and travel time to your destination. Include extra copies of your résumé and business cards in your briefcase. Don't forget paper for taking notes and a pen.

You are prepared. Now smile.

P is for practice, practice

If you followed the suggestions in Chapter 3, you took the time to identify your strengths and weaknesses, prepare questions you might expect in your interview, and actually practice or role-play your interview with a friend.

Realize too that unexpected things may happen in your interview process. No one can anticipate everything that will occur. But take confidence in the fact that you have practiced for a great deal of what will occur. And the fact that you are prepared and practiced in the skills of interviewing will give you the confidence you need to do well in the unexpected situations that may arise.

Imagine that you have just been certified in the RAPP school of confidence. You have done your research, you have taken care with your appearance, and you are prepared and well rehearsed. Those are strong reasons to go to the interview process with confidence.

You're On: Five Tips for Dealing with Stage Fright

Despite the confidence you know you should have because you are a graduate of the RAPP school, you know that you are going to feel nervous waiting for that interviewer's door to open. You may feel like your mind is a blank, your deodorant is not working, and you have forgotten how to speak. Never fear. What follows are five very simple strategies for dealing with the jitters even as you wait to be interviewed.

Tip #1: Take a deep breath

Sounds too simple to work, right? Try it. Take a deep breath. Hold it. Then consciously release your breath. Do this at least five times. By then you will feel that you are more in control of your breathing.

When your breathing is nice and regular, the pounding in your heart that tells you that you are really nervous takes comfort and calms down. When you concentrate on your breathing, you forget about some of the details that clutter your mind and shake your spirit.

Tip #2: Smile

You remember the old song, "Whenever I feel afraid. . . ." You will not be able to whistle a happy song in the interviewer's reception area or office, but you can smile. Medical research indicates that when you smile you exercise the muscles in your face, which actually helps you relax.

If you have never looked at yourself when you smile, go to that mirror again. Smile into the mirror. Smile until it feels natural and not artificial — not a goofy smile but a simple, pleasant smile. The worry lines in your forehead automatically go into hiding when you smile.

When you smile you elicit a more positive response from the person you're interacting with. Smile while you wait. Greet the receptionist and the interviewer with a smile. You and they will feel better about you.

Tip #3: Stretch

I'm not talking about a major workout here — just some simple things you can do in your chair while you wait for the interview to begin. All of them can be done unobtrusively while you sit in the reception area.

1. Close your eyes and rotate your neck in a full circle if possible. Do this clockwise twice and then counter-clockwise.

2. Press the palms of your hands together to feel isometric pressure. Hold the pressure for five seconds and release. Do it again until you feel more relaxed.

3. Pull in your abdomen muscles while you practice deep breathing. Hold your abdomen tight while you inhale deeply. Hold that breath for two or three seconds before exhaling. Relax your abdomen. Begin again.

4. Fold your arms across your chest and stretch your shoulder and neck muscles by pulling them outward and rotating them to the extent that you can do so unobtrusively.

Tip #4: Recognize the power of affirmations

Remember the story of the Little Engine That Could? He tackled a very difficult task and kept repeating the words "I think I can, I think I can" to help motivate himself and get his rhythm.

You too can send a positive message to yourself when you remember the story of that Little Engine. Repeat the words "I know I can, I know I can" until you find your rhythm and you believe what you are telling yourself.

You have every reason to believe that you will do well in this interview. And even if this interview does not result in this particular job, the skills and practice you gain here are a bonus for the next time.

Tip #5: Stay in touch

I remember going to a seminar, and the presenter made the comment that even if no one in the audience liked him or appreciated his remarks, he would still be loved and respected by his wife and that gave him the courage to continue.

Within those remarks lurks a lesson for everyone. You may feel nervous and alone waiting for that interview. Understandably, you do not want to disappoint yourself or your family or friends by messing up an interview. But the very people or person you do not want to disappoint is a great source of strength for you.

Go to your heart and touch base with a person who loves and respects you. That person has confidence in you. When you feel afraid or inadequate, you can connect with the energy and confidence of the person who supports you. Just say that person's name to yourself. You will feel calmed and more confident.

Being Realistic

One sure way to be nervous about an interview is to build it up into a monumental experience that would take a superhero to conquer. Do not make an interview a life or death kind of experience no matter how much you think you want a particular job, or how long you have been unemployed, or how desperate you feel.

Setting realistic goals for yourself and for this first interview are important to putting things in perspective. Your goals can include any of the following: Certainly you want to make a good impression on the interviewer, you want to get additional information about the particular job and the company, you want to be invited back for a second interview, and you would like to get some feedback about your status as a job candidate. (You may want to add your own goals to this list as well.)

If you accomplish these goals, your first interview will have been a success. You will have plenty of reason to feel good about yourself, your ability to handle the jitters, and your interviewing skills.

Making a good impression

Your entrance and your exit for the interview are probably the most important impressions you will make. Look at the following checklist and try to predict how the interviewer would evaluate you.

1. **Appearance.** How did you look? Did you appear confident, healthy, and informed?

2. **Body language.** Do your posture and gestures communicate self-assurance and ease with other people? Do you have annoying gestures or nervous habits? How's your handshake and smile?

3. **Mannerisms.** What do you do with your hands and feet when you are nervous? Are you aware of repeated gestures or facial expressions that might be annoying?

4. **Expressions.** What clichés do you often repeat as fillers or transitions? How often do you use them? Do you use "ah" and "uh" or "you know"?

5. Personal skills. How did you do with names? How will you try to remember people in the company? Did you come across as warm, competent, and comfortable with others?

Getting additional information

All the research you have done will not prepare you for the kind of job description the interviewer provides when you get to the interview. You should leave your first interview with a clearer idea of what the particular job entails and how it fits into the department and company goals and mission.

If you prepared questions to ask the interviewer, you may ask whether you may take notes to record responses and comments made during the interview. After the interview, you may incorporate these notes into your Company Fact Sheet so that all pertinent information is in one place.

After this first interview, both you and the interviewer have a better idea of the match between your experience and skills with the expectations for the job that was described in the interview. You may be convinced that you are perfect for the job, but the interviewer may have reservations and other candidates to interview. One of your jobs is to keep the door open for further discussions.

If you think the interviewer may have reservations about your experience and skills for the job, you might ask if you may take a proposal or assignment with you to demonstrate your ability to handle specific elements in the job description.

Getting a call back for a second interview

One of your goals in the first interview is to be invited to return for a second interview. As you conclude the first interview try to clarify the next steps. Ask the interviewer what kind of timeline the company has to fill the particular position. If you're asked to complete an assignment, be clear about when you are expected to have it completed and how you're to notify the interviewer.

Give the interviewer a reason to get back in touch with you. You might mention an informative article you read about the industry and offer to send a copy to the interviewer. Offer to develop a proposal for the company that deals with the type of assignment that you might be given if you were hired. Volunteer to work with somebody in the company who is struggling to meet a deadline while understaffed. Suggest that you work as a consultant for a limited period of time if that kind of arrangement is appropriate.

Remember

You're more likely to get a second interview if you give the interviewer a reason to get back to you because you are sending something or doing something that is perceived as a benefit.

Getting feedback

Have a strategy in place for getting feedback after your first interview. Your strategy might include sending a thank-you note within a day or two of the interview with the suggestion that you would like to talk with the interviewer to get some feedback on the interview process.

If the period of time specified by the interviewer passes without your hearing from the company, try calling the interviewer. Sometimes decisions are delayed, and reasons appear for not getting back to the job candidates. Ask if he or she can give you some feedback on your interview so that you can learn for the future. Most interviewers do not refuse that request, especially if you say that you have three questions. This limits the amount of time spent on this type of feedback session and takes pressure off the interviewer to defend the company's choice. He or she can be of some assistance to you even though the information you receive is not directly related to the position for which you interviewed.

Your feedback questions might include

1. How might I improve the general impression I make when I come to an interview?

2. What might I do to improve my background or skills to make me more suitable for this type of position? (Name the job for which you interviewed.)

3. Do you know someone inside or outside the company who might be interested in talking to me about my background and skills?

Armed with these suggestions, your first interview will be a winning situation for you. Good luck.

CHAPTER 5

MASTERING THE INTERVIEW: COMMUNICATING CLEARLY AND PERSUASIVELY

IN THIS CHAPTER

- Providing information and making transitions that help the interview process flow easily
- Developing a strategy for answering questions clearly and persuasively
- Communicating effectively with body language

You begin communicating the instant you walk into the receptionist's area to wait for the interviewer to open the door. If you make a bad impression on the receptionist, that impression may be passed on to the interviewer. Your goal, once you have arrived for the interview, is to communicate with everyone you meet clearly, positively, and persuasively.

Communication involves not only what you say but non-verbal messages, as well. In this chapter, you learn techniques for speaking clearly and persuasively. You also get some suggestions for communicating in a non-verbal way so that you leave a positive impression on those you meet.

When you pay attention to your verbal and non-verbal communication skills, you improve your chances for delivering a winning job interview.

Strategies for Beginning the Interview

Your first interview will probably take about one hour. At least three parts of your interview exist — the introductory "small talk," the questions and answers, and finally, the close.

Surviving small talk situations

The beginning of the interview should establish rapport, set the tone for the rest of the interview, and perhaps deal with small talk questions. In some cases, the "Tell me something about yourself" opportunity is used as the transition to the question-and-answer period of the interview.

Your interview probably begins with a remark or question considered "small talk." You certainly do not want to go on and on about the weather no matter how bad (or good) it might seem. Keep these remarks brief. Don't take over the interviewer's job by initiating small talk yourself. Be cordial, but wait for cues from the interviewer.

If the interviewer begins with something like "Did you have a hard time finding our office?" respond in such a way as to let the interviewer know that you did your homework and knew the directions. If you received assistance from someone in the office, let the interviewer know of the help you received from a particular person.

If you are interviewing in a city different from your home, take the time to read a local newspaper. The opening small talk may involve a comment about a local sports team or political situation. You want to be knowledgeable but avoid controversial opinions at all costs.

The interviewer may ask you what you would like to be called. The degree of formality or friendliness is often deter- mined by your response to this question. If your name is

James and no one calls you Jim just say that friends and acquaintances alike call you James. You then have the opportunity to ask how the interviewer would like to be addressed. Some prefer the Mr., Ms., or Mrs. title with their last name. Whatever name the interviewer prefers, find an opportunity to use it in direct address soon after these introductions are completed.

Remember

The interviewer sizes up your ability to communicate verbally and non-verbally in those important first minutes of an interview. Speak briefly and in a friendly manner. Do not give the impression that you are avoiding the real business of the interview.

You may be offered a drink during the introductory phase of the interview. Even though you may be eager for a cup of coffee or a glass of water, you aren't there to socialize; it's probably better to pass up this opportunity. Simply say, "No, thank you" and let the interviewer settle down to the business at hand.

Transitioning to the main part of the interview

The interviewer may steer into the main part of the interview with some variation on the request to "tell me something about yourself." Chapter 3 guides you to prepare a short and positive response to this request. Review those suggestions and practice your response.

The first part of the interview will be successful if you do the following:

- Make a good first impression with your appearance. (See Chapter 4.)

- Appear friendly and relaxed; smile and shake hands well.

- Practice the skill of making small talk and keep it brief.

- Avoid controversial comments or statements of opinion.

- Prepare a brief response to the "tell me about yourself" request.

Now that the first part of the interview has gone well, you can settle into the main part of the interview, handling the questions and answers pursued in the interview process.

Strategies for Questions and Answers

The second part of the interview focuses on the questions and answers exchanged between you and the interviewer. Typically, this part of the interview lasts between 30 and 40 minutes. Chapters 6, 7, and 8 help you deal with the basics of the interview process.

The final part of the interview is the close. This is the time when you learn about the company's timeline for making a decision about the position you are being interviewed for. Chapter 8 deals with strategies for dealing with this important time in the interview.

Consider the following strategies for handling the questions and answers part of the interview.

Choose your words carefully

Because the interviewer pays close attention to what you have to say, you want to choose your words with care. Select words that describe your skills and experience positively. Select words that imply a readiness to transfer to the job opportunity you are discussing in the interview.

Review the following list of words and phrases and identify those that best apply to you. These words represent skills that can transfer to any type of job. Check those that apply to you and find a way to work them into the responses you make to the interviewer's questions. You may want to use other words that represent your skills, as well.

_____ Meet deadlines _____ Helpful _____ Cheerful

_____ Conscientious _____ Creative _____ Mature

_____ Analytical _____ Independent _____ Tactful

_____ Mature _____ Loyal _____ Sincere

_____ Self-confident _____ Motivated _____ Efficient

_____ Problem-solver _____ Patient _____ Original

_____ Open-minded _____ Trustworthy

Be honest

The interviewer looks for appropriate disclosure and honesty in your responses to the questions asked during the interview. The interviewer has the right to know about your job history, your job performance, and your relations with supervisors and co-workers. The interviewer does not have the right to know personal issues regarding marital status, age, or other matters, which are discussed in Chapter 7.

Hiding information the interviewer has a right to know only leads to trouble. Do not conceal legal or financial problems that are work related. Avoid ambiguous responses to direct and legitimate questions. Always tell the truth and do not attempt to stretch it in an effort to make yourself look better than your record supports.

Responding to ethical questions with responses like "Everybody does it" or "It's just the way it is" conveys the impression that you are not always aboveboard and honest.

Common Interview Questions

Chapter 3 examined several of the most frequently asked questions in the interview process. The ten most commonly asked questions in an interview appear in the following list. This chapter suggests responses to those questions not treated in Chapter 3. (Chapter 3 suggests approaches to questions 1 through 4.)

1. Tell me something about yourself. (See Chapter 3.)

2. What are your strengths on the job? (See Chapter 3.)

3. What do you consider your weakness to be? (See Chapter 3.)

4. What are your career goals? (See Chapter 3.)

5. How does your previous experience relate to our current job opening here?

6. What do you think your former supervisor and co-workers would say about you?

7. Why should we hire you?

8. What salary expectations do you have?

9. What do you consider to be your best accomplishments at (previous company)?

10. Do you have any questions?

Previous experience

The interviewer wants to learn what you did in your previous job(s). More important, he or she makes a judgment about how those experiences might transfer to the job and corporate culture where you are interviewing.

Review the words you identified in the "Choose your words carefully" section. Choose five that best apply to you. Think of an example from your past job performance that illustrates each word or phrase that you selected from the checklist. You may want to write out one or two sentences for each transferable skill. Practice saying these sentences so that you're comfortable using the words and confident that you'll remember the response you can make to the question about past experience.

When you're asked about your previous experience, you'll be prepared to respond with concrete examples that use positive words suggesting that your past experience will transfer to a new job situation.

How others perceive you

Your response to this question gives the interviewer a good idea about your perception about the realities of the workplace. Remember, the interviewer can call your references to get "second opinions" about you.

Some strategies for responding to the question about what your boss and colleagues think of you include:

- Indicate that what they might think is revealed in words and behavior. Then provide examples of words or behavior that indicates the respect and recognition of others.

- If possible, quote some of the words used in your past performance evaluations to describe your attitude and achievements. If your past job evaluations have been positive, quoting from the report(s) conveys more substance than simply saying, "I got along well with my boss and co-workers."

- If you've been recognized as employee of the month or received some other award, certificate, or recognition, mention it now.

- As part of your preparation, consider asking former colleagues or managers to write a brief recommendation for you. Have copies with you, read an excerpt, and ask the interviewer whether you can leave or send copies for subsequent review.

Why should we hire you?

This question grants you the opportunity to speak persuasively. Think about the job skills you have and the positive, transferable skills you have identified. Now is the time to turn these skills into benefits for the company you are interviewing with.

Select three to five of your strongest points and best transferable skills. (Review Chapter 3 and the words you chose in "Choosing your words carefully.") Use the following example to complete the following worksheet. When the worksheet is complete, you will be able to identify strong benefits that the company will enjoy as a result of hiring you.

Example: **Transferable Strong Point:** I am reliable. Give me a job, and I will get it done well and on time. **Benefit to Company:** Management will have no surprises. Reliability translates into good time management — deadlines will be met. Reliability translates into staying on budget because no outside help will have to be called in at the last minute to help complete assignments. Reliability translates into quality assurance because the accepted performance standards have been implemented in the past.

1. Transferable Strong Point_____

Benefit to company _____

_____

2. Transferable Strong Point_____

Benefit to company _____

_____

3. Transferable Strong Point_____

Benefit to company _____

_____

4. Transferable Strong Point_____

Benefit to company _____

_____

5. Transferable Strong Point_____

Benefit to company _____

_____

You may want to add to these reasons why the company should hire you, but the truth is that the interviewer will not remember more than three reasons or benefits. If you prepare five reasons, you can select those that you think will have the most appeal to the particular interviewer.

Salary expectations

Chapter 10 discusses at greater length the issue of salary negotiation and your response to a question about salary. Just remember that if the interviewer is even remotely interested in you as a candidate for the job you are interviewing for, this question will come up. You cannot avoid answering this question. And your response is a good indicator of your knowledge of the industry and your skills as a negotiator. Don't skip Chapter 10.

Past achievements

When the interviewer asks you a question about the accomplishments you are most proud of, you can be prepared to respond in a way that suggests not only personal satisfaction but also measurable benefits to the company you work(ed) for.

The following worksheet helps you identify accomplishments that can be presented as not only personally satisfying but beneficial to the company as well.

Example: Challenge — I was asked to head up a development team to bring out a new electronic product for the company in less than six months. Benefit — as a result, the company generated additional revenue of $5 million in that fiscal year.

1. Challenge _____

Benefit _____

2. Challenge _____

Benefit _____

3. Challenge _____

Benefit _____

Do you have any questions?

This kind of question usually marks the transition to the conclusion of the interview. Even if the interviewer has been very
thorough and informative, having a couple of questions ready
to ask the interviewer is best. The questions you ask reveal
the level of information and intelligence you bring to the
interview.

Your response to the invitation to ask questions might include
any of the following:

■ What is the anticipated growth of the company over the
next five years?

■ How do you expect the position I am applying for to
change over the next couple of years?

■ What are your next steps in the process of selecting
someone to fill this job?

■ May I send you _____ (a list of references, a proposal,
an interview feedback form, and so on)?

Never ask whether you got the job or how you did in the
interview in response to the question, "Do you have any
questions?" Keep your questions focused on the company,
the job, and the subsequent procedures.

CHAPTER 6
ACTIVE LISTENING

IN THIS CHAPTER

- Paying attention to non-verbal communication
- Learning to listen well

Any job you apply for will involve good listening skills. You have the opportunity to demonstrate that skill in the interview process. Like most everything else, however, good listening skills just don't happen; they take work. Active listening requires that the listener receive both the speaker's spoken and unspoken message — which can be a difficult task. Too often the listener is so busy preparing a mental response to what the speaker is saying that he or she ignores much of the speaker's message, resulting in a less-than-perfect response. If you want to be an effective communicator, especially in the job interview process, you need to develop your active listening skills. Five tips for developing better listening skills follow.

Tip #1: Pay Attention

Paying attention is often harder to do than it sounds, especially in an interview when you want to remember all the things that you've practiced. Be confident that the skills you practiced before the interview won't desert you.

Give the speaker your full attention. Consciously reject the distractions that obscure what is being said. Stereotypes and negative judgements can interfere with your ability to listen objectively. Other distractions include the externals of the environment you're in. For example, the temperature in the room or the speaker's appearance can become distractions if you let them. In addition, you have all those distractions in your own head, including trying to plan your response to the speaker before the speaker has finished talking.

Some tips that you can use to focus your attention on the speaker include:

- Look at the speaker, focusing your attention only on the part of the room where the speaker is.

- Lean slightly forward in your chair to convey your interest and attention.

- Make a conscious decision to ignore the distractions in the room and in your head.

When you pay attention to the speaker in this way, your own response has more influence and impact because the interviewer recognizes that you've paid attention and really understand what was said.

Tip #2: Summarize What the Speaker Has Said

You can develop your listening skills by summarizing what the speaker has said. Too often listeners mentally finish what the speaker is saying and tune him or her out before the speaker is finished. When this happens, the listener often misses important points or the subtle messages of the tone or *feeling* of the message. If you want to practice tuning in to tone of voice, try saying "Come on" in a desperate tone, in a loving tone, in a hurt tone, and in an angry tone.

Learning to summarize what a speaker has just said is an important skill. When you can summarize what a speaker says to the speaker's satisfaction, you gain that person's respect and confidence. As a result, your own response has greater influence and impact.

Get in the habit of mentally or verbally summarizing what you've just heard. For example, when talking with your spouse, ask her whether you can try to repeat what you heard. Ask her to add any important points you missed. More often than not, what the speaker thinks you missed will amaze you!

You can also practice summarizing the information you hear by listening to the news. At each commercial break, try to itemize all the news stories covered in that segment. Do this exercise until you're fairly confident that you haven't omitted any. If you want to further enhance this skill, try to summarize the main points of each story.

Never try to complete the interviewer's sentences while he or she is speaking.

Tip #3: Take Notes

Taking notes while you listen is another strategy for becoming a better listener. Doing so when you are in an interview has several benefits:

■ Taking notes in an interview gives the interviewer a non-verbal message that you are serious and that you value what he or she is communicating.

■ Having these notes helps you raise significant questions when the interviewer asks, "Do you have any questions?"

■ Having these notes helps you with your follow-up communications because you can refer to specific comments or topics covered in the interview. The more specific and customized your thank-you follow-up is, the greater the chance it will make a favorable impression on the interviewer.

Warning

Although most interviewers respect your interest in getting accurate information, never take notes during an interview without first asking the interviewer's permission. Occasionally, interviewers find note taking to be a distraction.

A few suggestions for taking notes while you are in the interview are:

- **Ask the interviewer's permission.**

- **Be discreet.** Have a note pad and pen easily available. Don't make a big deal out of pulling a pad of paper from your briefcase.

- **Maintain eye contact.** Even while you take notes, keep looking at the interviewer. Don't let your body language give the impression that the note-taking process is more important than actually listening to the interviewer.

- **Don't let your notes become a distraction for the interviewer.** If they seem to distract the interviewer, stop. Let your notes be unobtrusive, out of the interviewer's direct sight. Just jot down key words or questions. Don't try to write in complete sentences.

- **Soon after the interview, review your notes to fill in the blanks and complete the thoughts that you simply jotted down in the interview.** You may want to label your notes with a code for "Good information," "Action," "Follow up," or whatever applies to your situation.

Tip #4: Ask for Feedback

You may think that you listen very well, but the speaker may disagree. If you are brave and prepared to make improvements, asking for feedback is an excellent way to find out how good your listening skills are.

The interviewer shouldn't be the first person you ask about your listening skills. You can get feedback in several ways. Try any of the following:

- Ask a good friend whether other people think that you're a good listener. Ask for suggestions about how to improve.

- After a business meeting, try to write a summary of the issues raised and points discussed in the meeting.

- Ask a friend to read an editorial from the paper or newsmagazine. Summarize both the information and the tone of the article.

Tip #5: Practice Makes Perfect

Active listening is not something you just decide to do one day. It takes time and practice. Just as you prepared responses to probable interview questions and prepared yourself mentally and physically for your big interview, you can also prepare to be a good listener. Practice is important. By improving your listening skills, you're more than halfway home to becoming a better communicator on the job (and at home).

CHAPTER 7

HANDLING DIFFICULT QUESTIONS AND SCENARIOS

IN THIS CHAPTER

- Knowing what a prospective employer can and can't ask in an interview

- Devising strategies for handling difficult and stressful interviews

Some interviews are particularly stressful because the interviewer asks really tough questions. In some cases, the interviewer may even ask illegal questions that violate the rights of the person being interviewed. In other cases, the person being interviewed is asked to describe performance in a variety of hypothetical and difficult work-related situations. Although preparing for really stressful interviews is difficult, knowing what to expect is one way to reduce such stress in an interview.

This chapter prepares you for difficult questions an interviewer may ask. You also learn what questions are out of bounds and shouldn't be asked or answered. In addition, this chapter describes some difficult scenarios that an interviewer may put you through as part of the interview process. Just knowing that this kind of interview can take place can help you appreciate the suggested strategies for dealing with them.

Illegal or Inappropriate Questions

Various federal and state laws and regulations influence the kinds of questions employers can ask in interviews. In general, interviewers avoid questions relating to religion, national origin, sex, age, race, or disabilities. Such questions can be used as part of a claim of job discrimination.

Check with your state's Fair Employment Practices Commission for a list of questions that are considered inappropriate in a job interview. You can find this contact information in the phone directory or on the Web.

Questions about race, religion, or ethnicity

Employers may not ask about your or your spouse's ancestry, nationality, or parentage. Suppose that an interviewer makes a comment like, "Your last name sure sounds Italian (or whatever)." Your response? Nothing. Simply smile politely and say nothing. Don't nod or in any way encourage that line of conversation or questioning. Other potentially libelous questions include

■ Where does your family come from?

■ That's an interesting last name. What nationality is it?

■ This company is Jewish (or Christian or Muslim or whatever). Would you be happy working here?

■ Where were you born?

■ That's an interesting accent. Where are you from?

These questions are illegal and shouldn't be asked or answered. Every question asked in an interview should relate to your current job or the one you're applying for. If it doesn't, the question is probably inappropriate and may be illegal.

Your strategy for dealing with such comments or questions involves tact, silence, and ingenuity — but not confrontation. Many times, you can respond to such questions with a polite smile and silence. You don't want to antagonize the interviewer with a harsh rebuff. In some situations, silence can also be provocative. If you think you must make some verbal response, say something like, "I don't see how my ancestry (or whatever) relates to my application for this job."

If an employer asks you to submit a photograph of yourself with your résumé or application, decline. An appropriate response is something like, "I don't have a recent photo available now. If I'm offered this job, I'd be happy to have one taken."

In general, avoid volunteering personal information that isn't related to your current job or the one you're applying for. Don't offer information about your age, ethnicity, or marital status. Instead, concentrate on information about your experience, education, and personal interests.

Questions about marital status and children

Interviewers may not ask questions about your marital status, plans for marriage, or plans for having children. You never know when the answers to these kinds of questions might be held against you when the company makes a hiring decision. Consider these representative situations to learn how to respond and what to avoid:

■ **Situation A. Are you married? Are you a family man (woman)? Would you like to be called Mrs. or Ms.?** Don't volunteer information on your marital status, whether you are planning to marry or not, or whether you have, or want to have, children. If asked how you'd like to be addressed, as Mrs. or Ms., suggest the use of your first name. This response avoids the marital designation of Mrs. or the feminist stance of Ms.

If you inadvertently refer to your spouse in the course of the interview, the interviewer can follow up with questions about the spouse, such as what he does or how she feels about your applying for this job. You can respond by refocusing the questioning on the job you're interviewing for.

■ **Situation B. Do you have children? Do you plan to have children? Who cares for your children?** In response to these sorts of questions, you should refocus the question to its impact on the job you're interviewing for. For example, you might say, "If you're asking about children because you want to assess my commitment to my career, let me assure you that the time and effort I have spent on establishing my career will not be replaced with domestic issues."

Be prepared to deflect the issues of children, childcare, and pregnancy and keep the questions focused on commitment to career and reliable past performance.

Questions about age, weight, health, or disabilities

These questions are almost always illegal because of the potential for discrimination charges. Employers may try to guess an applicant's age based on the time sequence that a résumé suggests. If an interviewer asks your age, you can respond in one of three ways: with humor, with the truth, or with silence. If you choose humor ("I'm old enough to know that I want this job") or simply state your age, be absolutely quiet after your response. No matter how long the silence, wait for the interviewer to say something. You will have the advantage here.

Companies have a legitimate interest in their employees' health because they offer health insurance and subsidize the premiums. Interviewers may only ask about conditions or disabilities that directly affect performance on the specific job you're interviewing for. The interviewer may not ask if you have an existing mental condition, received workers' compensation, problems with drugs or alcohol, or HIV or AIDS.

After you've been offered a job, however, the company may ask you to undergo a physical examination. If the results of the exam directly relate to job performance, the employer has the right to condition the job offer on those results.

Guidelines for handling illegal or inappropriate questions

Following are general tips for dealing with questions you shouldn't have to deal with:

- **Know your rights:** Be aware of illegal or inappropriate questions. Know in advance how you will respond.

- **Don't volunteer personal information:** The atmosphere may seem friendly and accepting, but you never know what information may be used against you.

- **Avoid confrontation:** Be polite, and learn to refocus the question to the job itself. Warn the interviewer in a subtle way that you're aware that the particular question seems inappropriate, but allow the interviewer to save face by rephrasing the question so that it relates to the job qualification.

- **Maintain a positive attitude:** Even though a question is inappropriate, the interviewer may be ignorant or inexperienced and unaware of the transgression. Unless the line of questioning is blatant and unrelenting, keep positive, shift the focus, and go on without taking personal offense.

Dealing with the Difficult Questions

Many interviews also include some "hardball" questions that are intended to put the person being interviewed on the spot. Rather than avoiding questions about your personal work history when that history contains some skeletons, prepare to deal with them honestly and with a positive attitude. Don't take offense at the question, but rather, try to understand what reservation the interviewer is expressing — even if that reservation has been expressed inappropriately.

This section considers three kinds of questions that can be difficult to answer if you aren't prepared.

Have you ever been fired? For what reasons?

People get fired for many reasons, including poor job performance, personality conflicts, clashes of management styles, restructuring within the company, company politics, or a change in upper management personnel. If you've ever been fired, do yourself the favor of stopping to think about the reasons. Knowing what went wrong is the first step in preventing it from happening again. Analyzing the situation is also essential if you want to give an adequate explanation in a job interview.

If you're asked about being fired from a previous job, your response should be honest, brief, and positive. For example, you may say something like, "My supervisor valued speed over quality in the completion of a critical product development. This difference led to my dismissal."

After giving a brief explanation, let it drop. If you can't give your past supervisor as a reference, think of someone else within the company who was an ally. Ask for a written reference in advance of the interview. If the interviewer asks you about being fired, you can then provide a positive reference from within the company, which can balance the negative impression often associated with getting fired.

Don't go into great detail in explaining why you were fired. Avoid negative comments about your past boss or company. You never know whether the interviewer has friends or contacts with your past employer.

Questions about being out of work

Most people find themselves out of work at some time in their professional careers. Some people land back on their feet quickly, but others sometimes take awhile. No matter how long you've been out of work, you don't want to come across as desperate in a job interview.

Plenty of good reasons exist for an extended job search. If you've been looking for a suitable job for a long time, take the time to figure out why. If a lengthy unemployment is related to your lack of preparation or training, you can do something about that. If you lack interviewing skills, this book can help you be better prepared.

If you've been out of work for a long time or if your work history contains significant gaps, be prepared to answer a tough question like, "Why are you still looking for a job?" Your response to that question may involve any of the following reasons:

■ **I'm searching for the right opportunity. I want to make the right choice and the right decision because I don't want to go through this process of finding a job again anytime soon.**

■ **I've had personal (or domestic) issues to deal with. As a result, I haven't had the time to give my full attention to getting a job.** State the issue briefly — the care of an elderly parent, settling the estate of a friend, and so on — so as not to invite further questioning along personal lines.

■ **The consulting assignments I've had have kept me busy.** Be ready to follow up this statement with a good example of work you've done for a specific industry without disclosing the actual name of the client.

■ **I have been getting further training (or education) to prepare me for this change of direction in my career.**

Questions about sexual harassment

Interviewers have the right to ask questions concerning sexual harassment. These questions can come in a variety of forms:

■ **Have you ever been accused of sexual harassment?** If you've been accused of sexual harassment but were exonerated, you can simply respond, "No." If you try to elaborate, you put yourself at the mercy of the interviewer who can ask a follow-up question that requests more details than you legally have to provide.

■ **Have you ever filed a sexual harassment complaint?** The interviewer may be interested in finding out your proclivity to take legal action in response to situation. Be careful of your answer. If you respond in the affirmative, you may make the interviewer more cautious about his or her decision to hire you. If you have filed such a complaint, you may want to consult your lawyer about the best response to this kind of question.

■ **Has a sexual harassment complaint been filed against you?** You don't need to incriminate yourself in response to this question. However, you do need to respond honestly. If this situation is part of your work background, prepare a careful response, perhaps with the assistance of your lawyer.

Handling Difficult Scenarios

Sometimes interviews aren't conducted in the traditional one-on-one format. Panel interviews, where several people are involved in the questioning, have become increasingly commonplace; you may be asked to participate in a behavioral interview; or you may be asked to respond to a situational interview.

Panel interviews

In a panel interview — common with government agencies and academia — several people interview you at the same time in hopes of eliminating the need for a second interview or to determine team dynamics. Typically, the interview consists of general introductions, small talk, and a round of questions from each of the panelists.

Following are tips for dealing with panel interviews:

■ **When first introduced to panel members, ask each of them for a business card, and arrange them in front of you to mirror the seating arrangement.** This way, you can always address an individual by name. The panelist's title also provides a clue to his or her interest in a specific question.

■ **Maintain good eye contact with the members of the panel.** Look directly at the individual asking a question but include glances around the panel as you answer the question.

■ **Be positive.** Look at the panel interview as an opportunity to win the attention of several people and demonstrate your people skills.

Behavioral interviews

Behavioral interviews are based on the belief that past performance is the best predictor of future success. This interviewing approach relies more on specifics. Questions usually begin with phrases like "Tell me about a time when . . ." or "Give me an example of . . . ."

Interviewers usually develop their line of questioning around the traits and skills they have determined are important for success in the position. For example, if being a team player is important, the interviewer may say, "Give me an example of how you participate on teams." If customer service is a necessary component of job success, the interviewer may say, "Describe your approach to dealing with annoying customers."

To prepare for behavioral questions, review your résumé with a fine-toothed comb and memorize some examples. Going through your résumé line-by-line gets you comfortable with how you plan to answer behavioral questions.

If you aren't a natural-born storyteller, prepare and edit your examples by using what career counselors call the D-A-R format:

■ DESCRIBE a specific project, task, or challenge you had to handle. (Obviously, you want to select examples that reflect positively on you.)

■ Explain the ACTION you took to respond to the task.

■ Identify the RESULTS or positive consequences of your action.

Situational interviews

In a situational interview, you're asked to perform a task that the interviewer believes is related to the job you're applying for. Several kinds of situational interviews exist:

- **Group Problem-Solving Situation:** In this situation, the interviewer may place you with two or three other applicants and a company representative. Working as a team, you are asked to solve a problem.

- **Priorities Situation:** In this situation, the interviewer may give you a box or basket containing memos, phone messages, appointment schedules, project schedules, and various papers you may expect to find on a manager's desk. You are asked to prioritize these items within a specified time period.

- **Role-Playing Situation:** The interviewer may ask you to role-play a situation in a fictitious setting. For example, if you're applying for a sales job, you may be asked to make a sales presentation, handle an employee, or deal with a complaint.

When dealing with problem-solving scenarios or hypothetical questions, coming up with the "right answer" is less important than communicating how you'd go about solving the problem. Take time to organize your thoughts — asking good questions can be more important than guessing at answers.

To deal successfully with situational interviews, consider these tips:

- **Recognize that actions speak louder than words.** In the case of situational interviews, the verbal responses you make may not matter as much as how you perform under stress or in "virtual" situations that mirror the company's real environment.

■ **Practice being in group discussions and participate actively.** If you're looking for a practice group, go to your local library or bookstore and join a book discussion group. Resolve to make at least one comment or ask one question at every meeting.

■ **Read specialized books or magazines that focus on interview techniques, including situational interviews.** Being prepared is a good way to reduce stress and learn to recognize what the interviewer is looking for in these interviews.

CHAPTER 8
CLOSING THE INTERVIEW

IN THIS CHAPTER

- Knowing when the interview is complete
- Selecting your last words
- Leaving a positive lasting impression

The conclusion of a first interview is very important. Just as your first impression sets the tone for the rest of the interview, you also want to leave a very positive and lasting impression. You want to have clear expectations about the future of this particular job prospect as well.

This chapter helps you prepare for an interview's conclusion. Your final words and questions influence the next steps in the process of securing a winning job interview. (Interviewers rarely extend a job offer at the end of a single interview. Therefore, a winning job interview doesn't end until you actually start your new job.) This chapter also suggests strategies for closing the first interview on a positive note, with opportunities for further contact that could lead to a second interview.

Recognizing the End of the Interview

Interviewers almost always give signals via words and body language that the interview is coming to a close. When you recognize these clues, they provide you with an opportunity to raise a significant question, suggest a callback strategy, and summarize key points made in the interview.

However you get the signal that the interview is about to end, you will probably have one more opportunity to ask a question or make a comment. This final comment is as important as your first impression because it reinforces the interviewer's impression of you.

Closing statements made by the interviewer

The interviewer can use direct or fairly subtle statements to begin the conclusion of the interview. If using a direct approach, the interviewer may say something like, "That just about covers the material I wanted to talk about. I think I have a pretty good idea of the experience and skills you would bring to this position. We're interviewing several other candidates over the next two weeks. I'll get back to you after we've seen them. We appreciate your coming to see us." When you hear these or similar words, the interview is over, and you have your signal to make a transition to your closing question or remarks.

You also don't want to miss the more subtle words that interviewers sometimes use to signal the conclusion of an interview. The interviewer may say things like

- "Well, we certainly covered a lot of ground today."
- "I think we've taken care of just about everything."
- "Do you have any other appointments today?"

These, too, are signals for you to make your transition to your closing question or comment.

Non-verbal clues

Some interviewers are not as direct in their attempt to conclude the interview. Most interviews only last between 30 to

60 minutes. The amount of time you've already spent in the interview process is a clue that the time to conclude the interview is at hand.

The actions or gestures the interviewer makes are additional clues that the interview is about to end. The following are common clues:

- The interviewer glances at the wall or desk clock or peeks at a wristwatch.

- The interviewer opens his or her appointment calendar and begins checking for other appointments.

- The interviewer begins to straighten papers or items on the desk.

When you observe any of those actions, take the opportunity for a reality check. Ask the interviewer, "How are we doing for time?" or "Is our time just about up?" or "Do we still have a few minutes? I have a question I'd like to ask."

Do you have any questions for me?

Most interviewers ask this or a similar question. Review Chapter 5 for suggestions about appropriate questions you may want to ask. Be flexible, though. During the course of the interview, you may realize that you want further clarification on something the interviewer said, in which case your pre-prepared questions should fall to the wayside. In any case, the burden is on you to ask a significant question that reflects your understanding of the position.

If you think the interview has gone well and you've established a good rapport with the interviewer, consider either of the following questions as possible transitions to the conclusion of the interview:

- What do you especially like about this company?

- What additional information may convince you to hire me for this job?

Speaking Your Last Words

You want to accomplish at least five things in your final comments and good-bye:

- Thank the interviewer, using his or her name.

- Express your interest in the company and in the job.

- Mention that you have a busy schedule.

- Arrange a reason to get back in touch with the interviewer.

- Say "Thank you" and "Good-bye."

Some people borrow closing techniques from the world of sales using, for example, the "Ben Franklin close," in which the candidate makes a point-by-point comparison of candidate qualifications versus employer needs. Whatever type of closing you choose, don't leave these important final words to chance. The following worksheet can help you organize your thoughts and plan a reason for continuing to stay in touch with the interviewer.

Take time to complete the following worksheet. The reasons for continued contact may vary depending on the nature of the interview. Look at the example provided and develop a response that works best for you and the particular job for which you are interviewing.

1. **Use the interviewer's name.**

Example: (While getting up to shake hands, say) "Mr./Mrs./Ms. ___, I am very grateful for your time today."

Write your own response: _____

_____

2. **Express interest in the company, product, job, and so on.**

Example: "I enjoyed our conversation today and am impressed with all that (company name) is doing. I am definitely interested in becoming a productive member of this team."

Write your own response: _____

_____

_____

3. **Mention your schedule.**

Example: "You said you will continue to interview candidates over the next two weeks, and I will be busy next week as well."

Write your own response: _____

_____

4. **Arrange for continued contact.**

Your objective is to have a reason to get back in touch with the interviewer. Reasons may include a) desire to send an additional copy of your résumé; b) interest in sending the interviewer a reference, an article, or some additional information mentioned during the interview; c) desire to get an answer to a question; or, d) need to submit a requested proposal or assignment.

Example: "I'm sure that I will have a question (or, I will want to contact you with the name of the person, article, or organization we spoke of). When would be the best time to call?"

Don't ask a question that the interviewer can answer with a "no," such as "May I call you on Monday?" You don't want to give the interviewer an easy way to get out of further contact.

Write your own response: _____

_____

5. **Make your exit.**

Example: "Thanks again, Mr./Mrs./Ms. _____. I look forward to talking with you soon."

Write your own response: _____

_____

Completing this worksheet each time you prepare for an interview helps you end the interview with a strong conclusion, as well as gives you an additional opportunity to contact the interviewer and leave another favorable impression.

Strategies for Lasting Impressions

Besides feeling relief at the end of an interview, you'll probably want to mentally review everything you said — and everything you wish you'd said. Following are some strategies for leaving a favorable last impression with the interviewer and for evaluating your performance at this interview to make improvements for the next one.

One last impression on the interviewer

After your final remarks, the final impression the interviewer will have is related to your handshake, your smile, and your walk out the door. You want these gestures to be positive.

Keep your handshake firm and your smile pleasant and genuine. If you want, pause before extending your hand and smiling. In that moment of pause, you can touch base with a positive image or thought. Convey that positive energy through your handshake and smile.

Your walk out the door should also convey optimism, energy, and enthusiasm. Your walk can tell the interviewer that the conversation and information about the company and its prospects energized you. As you approach the door, turn toward the interviewer and ask whether you should leave the door open or closed. This tactic gives you another opportunity to smile as you maintain eye contact.

Out the door

At this point, you want continued contact and a return for a second interview. (Chapter 11 tells you what to do to follow up on a final interview.) After you leave a first interview, you need to do a couple of things quickly:

■ **Write a brief summary of the interview you just had:** Include the name(s) and title(s) of those to whom you spoke. Use the following worksheet to help you summarize the important parts of the interview and identify the action items you want to pursue.

Name of company: _____

Name of interviewer(s): _____

Names of others (receptionist, secretary, and so on):___

_____

Date of interview_____

Significant information: _____

_____

_____

Action items and dates completed

1._____

2._____

3._____

Follow-up calls, notes with dates

_____

Things I think went well:

_____

_____

Things I think I can improve:

_____

_____

■ **Make a list of action items you want to pursue as a
result of the interview:** Include a thank-you note or letter to each person you talked with, including the receptionist or secretary if possible. (See Chapter 11 for
samples.)

You're ready to prepare for your second interview, so head on
over to Chapter 9.

CHAPTER 9
GETTING THE SECOND INTERVIEW

IN THIS CHAPTER

- ■ Retaining a positive image with the interviewer
- ■ Maintaining your networks within the company and industry
- ■ Preparing for a second interview
- ■ Clarifying expectations for a second interview

When the first interview goes well and you think that the interviewer is interested in you as a candidate for the position, you can begin to work for a second interview. Like the first interview, a second interview benefits from preparation and practice.

This chapter identifies several steps that you can take immediately after the first interview to enhance your visibility with the interviewer and reinforce the positive impression you made during the first interview. In addition, this chapter gives you practical suggestions for preparing for a second interview.

Appropriate Responses to the First Interview

After your own debriefing when the first interview is over (see Chapter 8), you can do at least three things to improve your chances for a second interview — and ultimately, employment:

- Express your gratitude for the interview with a thank-you note and phone call.

- Re-establish contact with your network(s) inside the company and within the industry.

- Prepare your references for a call from the interviewer.

Expressing your gratitude

Immediately follow up an interview with a written note or letter expressing your gratitude. You may also decide to make a telephone call. In either case, you want the follow-up call or note to accomplish five things:

- Help the interviewer remember your name and the date of the interview

- Restate one key qualification you have for the job

- Reinforce your continued interest in the job

- Clarify the next steps in the interview process

- Express gratitude for the interviewer's time and interest in your candidacy

If you decide to make a follow-up phone call, you must be prepared for several possibilities:

- The interviewer may not be available, and you will be transferred to voice mail.

- The interviewer may screen calls, which means that you may only speak to the gatekeeper or secretary.

- You may actually speak to the interviewer and learn that either no decision has been made or that you didn't get the job.

Use the following worksheet, customizing the script as appropriate, for your follow-up call:

Step 1: Clearly identify the specifics of the interview.

Hello, Mr./Ms. (Name). This is **your name**. We met last week, on **day and date**, to discuss my qualification for the position of **give job title**.

Step 2: Restate your key qualification.

Your preference for a candidate with recent training in **give example (such as computer-based project management experience)** is certainly related to my responsibilities as **name specific example**.

Step 3: Reinforce your continued interest in the position.

I am very interested in this position with **name of company**.

Step 4: Clarify the next steps.

Can you tell me where you are in the interviewing process?

(If no decision has been made, say something like, "I'm happy to learn that. Do you have additional questions for me at this time? When do you suggest that I call again?")

(If you learn that a decision has been made and you didn't get the job you may say, "I appreciate your time and consideration. If you need anyone with my qualifications in the future, I would certainly like to hear from you." If you think the interview went well and the interviewer is making encouraging remarks, you may solicit feedback by asking, "Do you have any suggestions to help me improve my interviewing skills?")

_____

_____

Step 5: Express gratitude.

I certainly enjoyed talking with you and appreciate the time you spent with me. I look forward to meeting with (or talking to) you again.

_____

_____

Even if you learn that you didn't get the job, you can use a telephone follow-up as an opportunity to reinforce the impression that you're a person of skill and character and to ask for further networking contacts. For example, you may say something like, "Because you know of my qualifications, do you know someone else who may be interested in talking with me?"

If, on the other hand, you are encouraged by your telephone follow-up, record the date of this call on your interview information sheet (see Chapter 7) and make a note for another follow-up call.

After every interview, you should send a brief note or letter of thanks to the person who interviewed you. The letter should accomplish the same things that the follow-up phone call does. The following shows a sample thank-you letter, which you can modify to suit your particular circumstances.

Be absolutely sure that you spell the names of the interviewer and company correctly. If you have any doubt, call the person who helped arrange the interview for assistance.

Your Address

Date

Mr. Fred Smith
Information Systems Manager
McMasterFoster, Inc.
1599 Farwell Ave.
Shorewood, WI 53211

Dear Mr. Smith:

Thank-you for the time you spent with me on Wednesday, August 15 discussing the position of Technical Information Coordinator and other projects at McMasterFoster. My recent certification in Program Apollo from the Acme Technical Institute is directly related to the skills required of the TIC as you described them in our interview.

I remain very interested in working at McMasterFoster as the Technical Information Coordinator. You indicated that the interview process would continue for several weeks. I will call you the week of June 15th to inquire about the status of this process.

Your assistance and encouragement are very much appreciated, and I look forward to speaking with you again.

Sincerely,

Anna Farley

Informing your networking contacts

Get in touch with the personal networking contacts that you made within the company and its industry after the interview. Just reporting an interview to your network contacts makes them feel more involved and inclined to help.

Use your network contacts to gain valuable feedback and insight into the interviewing process. Review the interview with each and ask, "What could increase my chances for a second interview?" You may also want to ask for suggestions about your next step in the pursuit of that job.

Alerting your references

An interviewer may ask you for references, so be prepared with a list of three people who have agreed beforehand to serve as business references for you. These references should be people who have worked with you or know you professionally. Your list of references should not include family, relatives, or friends.

When you begin the job-searching process, make a list of people you can use as references. Always secure their permission to use their names and contact information with a potential employer. If an interviewer asks for references, you can do the following after the interview:

■ **Ask the interviewer if you may mail or fax the list of references:** Ask how many references the interviewer would like you to supply. On a single sheet of paper, include all your references' names, addresses, phone numbers (home and/or business with preferred hours of contact), fax numbers, and e-mail addresses. On the same sheet of paper, include your name, contact information, and the title of the position for which you're applying.

■ **Contact your references after the interview to alert them to the possibility of a call from the interviewer.**

■ **Give your references the information they need to make relevant remarks about your experience and your job search:** Give each reference the name of the company and interviewer and the title of the position you've applied for.

Don't give your current boss as a reference unless you're willing to have that person know that you're job hunting. If the interviewer asks whether he or she can contact your current boss for a reference, respond along the following lines, "After I'm offered the job, I see no reason why that could not happen. Until the job is offered, though, I'd like the confidentiality of the interview process to be honored."

Second Interviews

Most companies will call you back for a second interview before making a final decision about you as a job candidate. These second interviews can take several forms. In a *serial interview,* you're passed from one person to the next within the organization. Another type of second interview — the invitation to a meal — is more informal, but just as important.

The serial interview

The purpose of the serial interview is to get a group assessment of your qualifications before the company makes a final decision about your application. Most likely, you'll meet supervisors, and perhaps peers, in the department you'd be working in. You may also meet the department's vice president, and you may talk with a human resources representative.

One of the dangers of the serial interview is that you can begin to feel like a robot mechanically reciting lines. Treat each interview as if it's the first, beginning with the need to establish rapport, build trust, and show both enthusiasm and responsiveness.

Every person you talk with during a serial interview basically has two concerns:

1. Can you do the job?

2. Will I want to work with you?

To deal with the first concern, remember that these people usually aren't professional interviewers. They're more comfortable with the actual conditions in the workplace. They'll want to hear about your work experience and your approach to solving problems or responding to challenges.

Be careful about discussing changes that you would want to make if you were hired. Instead, stress your willingness to learn from the department's past successes. Don't brag or alienate anybody.

The second concern is unspoken but real. Each person you speak with sizes you up mentally. You, in turn, must try to be sensitive to each person's communication style. Be alert to the clues that the interviewer gives. If someone seems to want to talk about your last job, share some anecdotes. If another wants to complain about the lack of job training in the department you'd be working for, listen and respond with an anecdote. For example, you may share how you or a subordinate in a previous job made a sale (or soothed a customer, acquired a new account, and so on) as a result of a training session you gave or attended.

You want to come across as a good, easy-to-work-with person. If you feel nervous about your ability to do so, Chapter 4 offers some helpful relaxation strategies.

The meal interview

When an interviewer suggests that you meet in a more informal setting for lunch or dinner, a great deal is at stake. The interviewer may invite several others to join you. In this setting, those at the table are more interested in the "Will we want to work with you?" concern than in pursuing your qualifications. They have probably already decided that you're qualified for the job. Following are a few tips for interviewing successfully over a meal:

1. **Eat and drink in moderation.**

If you're meeting at lunch, pass on the alcoholic beverages. Don't spend too much time looking over the menu. Make a simple choice quickly to exemplify your decision-making skills. Remember, even though you're in a restaurant, the primary purpose of this meeting is not to eat and drink.

2. **Keep the conversation friendly but focused on the job.**

The interviewer may take advantage of the meal's informal setting to try to gain information that would be awkward, inappropriate, or illegal to ask in the formal interview process. (For help in handling difficult questions, review Chapter 7.) If the interviewer makes a comment about his or her own family, know that you're being encouraged to share information about your marital status, family situation, or childcare arrangements. You may feel pressured to reveal more than you want to, so before you go to such a meeting, be very clear with yourself about how much personal information you're comfortable sharing.

Prepare your responses to anticipated questions carefully. For example, if you're engaged and the interviewer asks about your wedding plans, understand that your response is the basis for a judgment about how much time and energy you will devote to the job. Such a question is not a purely friendly query. Simply say something like, "We're well-organized and everything is falling into place," and then make a transitional remark that inquires about the major events the company anticipates in the near future.

3. Sell yourself.

This kind of interview puts a premium on compatibility and interpersonal skills. You can take some satisfaction in the fact that the interviewer has already determined that you're qualified for the job. Now is the time to sell yourself, so you want to be friendly and relaxed.

Just like any other sales presentation, emphasize the benefits you bring to the team and to the company. Based on your evaluation of the first interview, make a list of three things that you think the company is looking for in a successful job candidate. Review your own list of strengths (see Chapter 3) and match a strength with each of the three items on the company's wish list. Be prepared to state your strength as a benefit for the company.

For example, say you think that the company wants someone to manage their customer relations more economically, and your strength is record keeping. Your benefit statement may be, "I'm known as a good record keeper. I can develop a form for you that would help the customer service reps focus on the customer's issue while reducing the amount of time they spend on the phone with individual customers. That way, they'd have more time to remedy customer concerns."

In most cases, the purpose of the second interview is to assess the intangible quality of compatibility. After that concern is resolved, you can expect serious questions about salary and benefits.

CHAPTER 10

NEGOTIATING SKILLS IN THE INTERVIEW PROCESS

IN THIS CHAPTER

- Developing skills for negotiating salary, benefits, and those little extras
- Researching realistic salary expectations
- Recognizing what you're worth and getting it
- Knowing the right time to negotiate salary

Knowing how to negotiate a salary at the right time in the interview process can be worth thousands of dollars to you. And over time, a better starting salary can compound into significant money. As management speaker Suzanne Greene has said, "We spend years in school. We spend a large sum of money getting that education. We spend hours writing résumés and cover letters and interviewing. But when we finally get to the last detail — money, perks, and benefits — we usually negotiate this in less than five minutes."

This chapter can help you overcome any apprehension about discussing salary. You discover strategies for developing strong negotiating skills and find suggestions for learning about competitive salaries to help you determine your own worth in the market place. Finally, this chapter shows you the importance of timing when the subject of salary comes up.

Learning What You're Worth

Preparation is the key not only to a winning job interview but also to salary negotiation. The question about salary expectations always comes up in the interview process. Your response to the question involves preparation, skill in negotiating, and having some influence on the question's timing.

Despite the fact that information about personal salaries is confidential, information about salary expectations for many careers is available with a little research.

Sources of information

Your local library should have some of the readily available resources about median salaries and salary ranges in the most common occupations. Take a look at any of the following. Some offer general information about many industries; others specialize in segments of the American economy:

- **Occupational Outlook Handbook and America's Top 300 Jobs:** Both of these books contain information based on the U.S. Department of Labor. Both include information about starting salaries and average pay for about 85 percent of the workforce.

- **Career Guide to America's Top Industries:** This reference presents information for around 60 industries. You'll see that some industries pay better than others do.

- **America's Federal Jobs:** This government resource provides information about the types of federal jobs available and their requirements and salary ranges.

- **American Salaries and Wages Survey:** Published by Gale Research, this document provides data about thousands of jobs. The survey is organized geographically and gives cost-of-living information for selected areas.

- **American Almanac of Jobs and Salaries:** Avon Books publishes this almanac, which provides useful information about professional jobs, wages, and trends.

Other published sources that give information about specific industries and locales are also available. Your local library can help you access this more specialized information.

Experience is a good teacher

In addition to the wage research you do, your own experience and professional associations are other sources of useful information as you prepare to negotiate the best salary you can.

If you're looking for your first job, you don't have a salary history. But knowing what's common to the industry can help you set realistic expectations and negotiate a competitive salary.

If you're applying for a job in the industry you have worked in for some time, you have a pretty good idea of what your skills and experience are worth — unless you think that you're grossly underpaid. The professional journals published in your career area often contain survey information about median salaries.

In addition, your network contacts can be a source of information about salaries. Of course, people won't tell you their individual salaries, but most feel comfortable talking about trends in the industry and salary ranges.

Be cautious with contacts that seem to reveal too much about personal salary or bonuses. Sometimes these people inflate figures in an effort to impress you.

Timing the Salary Question

In many cases, the interviewer asks the salary question early in the interview. In some cases, the question is raised even before the actual interview. A classified ad can indicate that your response must contain information about salary history or expectations. Or the initial telephone call can raise the question of salary in order to get the information the interviewer needs to screen out candidates who are outside the company's budget.

Questions about pay in the early stages of interviewing are aimed at either eliminating you from consideration because your expectations are too high, or saving money for the company at your expense because you are content with too little. Don't let either happen to you.

Strategies for delaying the discussion of salary

If a classified ad requires that you state your salary history, you can do a few things:

■ Take your chances and ignore the requirement. In this case, the company may reject you without any further consideration; then again, your résumé may be so outstanding that the interviewer will want to talk with you despite your omission.

■ Indicate that your present salary is competitive with industry standards.

■ If you've done your research, simply indicate a salary range that is common to the position.

In all cases, try to avoid the discussion of actual salary expectations until you've been offered the job and are in a position to negotiate a salary.

If an interviewer raises the "What is your current salary?" question, you should respond directly. Know that the interviewer will use your response to figure a negotiating position when you come to talk about salary. If you feel that your current salary is competitive, you can give the actual figure. If you feel that your salary is rather low, you can give a range, like "the mid-forties," rather than reveal the actual lower-end amount. If your salary is on the low side but your bonus or additional compensation is pretty good, you can say, "Last year, my total compensation was $75,000" (or whatever).

If the interviewer asks, "What salary do you expect?" early in the interview, try to avoid answering the question before an actual job offer is made. Keep in mind, however, that you must not come across as evasive or stubborn.

■ **You can answer the question with another question.** For example, you can ask the interviewer, "What salary range does (name of company) offer for positions with similar experience and training?"

Keep this question/response non-personal. Don't ask, "What do *you* pay for comparable experience?" Instead, ask in the name of the company. The interviewer can respond more easily if you ask about a range.

■ **You can answer the question with the suggestion that the salary can be negotiated, but not at the moment.** For example, you can say, "I'm very interested in this position, and my salary would be negotiable." Or, "I'm very interested in this position, and I'm sure that we can come to an agreement about compensation." This kind of response lets the interviewer know that you want to stay in the ball game but implies that a job offer should be made before the actual salary discussion.

■ **You can try to put the ball back in the interviewer's court.** For example, you may say something like, "I'm very interested in this position and would consider any reasonable offer (name of company) might make." Everything hinges on the word *reasonable;* and you're inviting the interviewer to offer an example of what *reasonable* means to that company.

If the interviewer persists, and you can't delay the salary expectation question further without seeming rude, then rely on the research you've done. Respond by giving a salary range within the industry's norms — with the upper end of the range slightly above what you think you can negotiate.

The timing is right: You've been offered the job

After the job has actually been offered and the interviewer has had reasonable assurance that you'll be able to negotiate a satisfactory salary and benefit package, the time is right to talk money.

As Suzanne Greene mentions in the quote at the beginning of this chapter, you've spent a great deal of time, effort, and money to get to this very important question; don't blow your response to the money question away in a matter of seconds. Use any of the following negotiating techniques after you've been offered the job.

Five Tips for Negotiating Salary and Benefits

You can do many things to develop strong negotiating skills. The following are just five tips for negotiating a salary and benefit package that will make you and your employer happy.

Tip #1: Give yourself confidence and enthusiasm

After the job is offered to you, you know that the company thinks highly of you and that it wants you to be a part of the team. You want to start the process of negotiating a salary and benefit package from a position of psychological strength. Have a positive attitude toward both the process and the outcome. Allow yourself the confidence and enthusiasm that come from a job well done.

Your confidence comes from the fact that you've done a good job of selling yourself and your experience to the interviewer. Continue to sell yourself to the company. Emphasize the benefits you can provide the company in terms of increased productivity, your creativity, your contacts and networks, your experience, or whatever you bring to the position. Let the employer know that you really like the company, the people, and the job. Your enthusiasm will be contagious.

You are wanted.

Tip #2: Let them make the first offer

Before the interviewer ever gets to the point of actually discussing a job offer, you have probably already fielded the salary expectation question, and a salary range is on the table. Be patient and let the company make an actual offer. Don't jump in and bring up the salary question first.

The impatient negotiator is at a disadvantage. Let the company make the first offer after you have given some idea of salary range. Never be the first to bring up money.

Tip #3: Enhance your compensation package

Salary isn't the only issue at stake when you negotiate a job offer. Most businesses offer a variety of benefits that often equal 40 percent of the actual salary. Before you agree on a salary, inquire about the benefits the company offers its employees. Listen carefully to all that the interviewer enumerates.

Typical benefits include the following:

- Bonus, incentives, and stock options
- Tuition reimbursement
- Paid vacation and sick time
- Flexible hours
- Family leaves
- Insurance, including health, life, and disability
- Profit sharing, 401(k)s, and retirement programs
- Employee discounts

As part of your negotiating strategy, ask for some benefits that you're willing to forgo. In some cases, you may be able to trade a benefit for a higher salary if salary is more important to you.

Salary is only part of your compensation. Negotiate the benefits to give yourself a better package.

Tip #4: Give yourself time

No matter how inviting or how disappointing a compensation package you're offered, ask for at least 24 hours to consider the offer. Much can happen in that in-between time you ask for. Remember, they want you.

In the intervening time, the company may decide to take a hard line and not negotiate further. The interviewer may not have room to negotiate. Remember, however, that even though the company is unable or unwilling to negotiate salary, it still wants you. The job offer still stands. In this kind of situation, you have to decide whether you want the job with a salary you're not especially happy about, or you prefer to keep looking for a job and a salary more to your liking. Sometimes, the choice is difficult.

In the time you give yourself for reflection, you want to accomplish the following:

■ Sort out your options as you reflect.

■ Plan your response carefully.

■ Make a comfortable decision about accepting the offer, making a counteroffer, or rejecting the offer.

Even if you decide to accept the offer quickly, wait out the time you have agreed on before informing the company of your decision. If you are inclined to make a counteroffer, be clear about your priorities and leave room for trading a benefit or salary adjustment to accomplish what you want. Never issue an ultimatum to a prospective employer such as, "If I don't get such-and-such a salary offer from you by next week, I will go somewhere else."

If you decide to reject the offer, do so graciously. Try to keep the interviewer and other people you talked with in the company in your network of professional contacts. Someone within your network may make a job change, or the work situation at the company may change, and you'll renew contact with the interviewer or company again. Remember the old adage: "Don't burn your bridges."

Tip #5: Get it in writing

Asking the interviewer to put the job offer and the employment package in writing is always a good idea. This strategy leaves little room for misunderstanding and gives you something concrete to negotiate from should you want to make a counteroffer. Ask that the interviewer include such items as first performance review, expected compensation adjustments, and the job description in the written offer. Your time for reflecting on the job offer begins after you receive this written statement.

The art and skill of negotiating is something that improves with practice. Just remember that when you are prepared and clear about your objectives, you can usually improve your position.

CHAPTER 11

FOLLOWING UP

IN THIS CHAPTER

- Preparing a letter of acceptance
- Notifying your present employer
- Maintaining your networks
- Transitioning to a new job

Even after you have accepted a job offer and concluded your winning job interview, you still have some loose ends to tie up. You need to follow up your verbal acceptance of a job offer with a letter of acceptance. In addition, you need to prepare a letter of resignation from your previous employer, and finally, you need to inform your network and thank each contact for the roles he or she played in offering support and guidance for your job search.

Composing Letters of Acceptance or Rejection

Your decision to accept a job offer involves evaluating the substance of the offer. Before you take a look at what to say in your acceptance letter, take a look at a typical job offer letter and the areas you should consider before accepting it.

What to look for in a written job offer

When you receive that written job offer, look for several things:

- **Job title and description:** You want to be clear about the position you are being considered for, especially if the interviewer mentioned several open positions in the company.

- **Salary and start date:** You have moved past the salary range discussion to the moment of truth: The actual figure suggested for your salary probably rests somewhere in the middle of the range you and the employer discussed.

- **Identification of special benefits that apply to your offer:** If your acceptance involves relocating to another city, the offer should include mention of relocation reimbursement procedures. If the job requires you to pass a physical or other type of test, that information needs to be specified in the letter. If a special benefit is connected to the offer — tuition reimbursement or flextime, for example — the letter should specify that, too.

- **An invitation to get back to the person extending the job offer if you have questions.**

- **A timeline for responding to the offer.**

With this type of job offer in hand, you need to reflect and evaluate the offer. Consider the ten-point checklist shown in Table 11-1 to help you decide whether this is the job for you.

Table 11-1: Job Offer Checklist

Rating	Job Characteristics
1 2 3 4 5	Do I really want to do this type of work?
1 2 3 4 5	Does this company and/or this job offer good opportunities for advancement?
1 2 3 4 5	How much do I like my immediate supervisor?
1 2 3 4 5	Does the company culture suit my personality?
1 2 3 4 5	How happy is my family with this choice?

Rating	Job Characteristics
1 2 3 4 5	Is this a good location for me?
1 2 3 4 5	Does the company and/or the job provide additional training opportunities?
1 2 3 4 5	Is the benefit program satisfactory?
1 2 3 4 5	What is my comfort level with this job?
1 2 3 4 5	Is this job a good choice for me now and in the future?

Sample acceptance letter

If you decide to accept the job as outlined in the written offer you receive, then you need to confirm the major aspects of your agreement in your own letter of acceptance. The following is a sample acceptance letter.

Your name
Your address
Date

Mr. Sergio Hernandez
ABC, Inc.
1234 First Street
Somewhere, IL 60025

Dear Mr. Hernandez:

I was delighted to receive your offer of the Systems Analyst position and want to confirm my acceptance of that position with this letter. ABC, Inc. and the people I have met are impressive and I am eager to join you in making a significant contribution to the business.

As indicated in your letter of June 15, I understand that I will start on September 5, with a starting salary of $50,000. I especially appreciate the tuition reimbursement benefit for the state certification program. I am enclosing the completed medical form that you requested.

I look forward to working with you and ABC, Inc.

Sincerely,

Your Name

Enc.

If, after reflecting on and evaluating the job offer, you decide not to accept it, you need to send a rejection letter that also conveys your appreciation for the offer. The following is a sample letter of rejection.

Your name
Your address
Date

Mr. Sergio Hernandez
ABC, Inc.
1234 First Street
Somewhere, IL 60025

Dear Mr. Hernandez:

Thank you for your offer to join ABC, Inc. as a System Analyst. I have given this offer a great deal of thought and have appreciated your time and consideration, but I have decided to decline the offer.

The opportunities at ABC, Inc. are truly impressive and I have great respect for those I have met within your organization. However, at this time, I have decided to pursue another course of action.

I want to thank you for extending this offer to me and for the confidence you have expressed in my experience and skills. Your professionalism and many courtesies are deeply appreciated.

Best wishes,

Your name

You don't need to explain why you're declining a job offer, but you can indicate a reason if you wish. The tone of your rejection letter depends on the degree to which you want to stay in touch with the interviewer or the company.

This kind of letter requires tact and courtesy. Avoid any hint of criticism or negativity.

Writing a Letter of Resignation

Only after you have received and accepted a written job offer should you prepare your letter of resignation from your present employer. Mix-ups and misunderstandings have been known to occur in the interviewing and negotiating process, so don't resign until you are absolutely sure about the details of your new employment.

Before your resign

In some cases, you will have shared your job search with some trusted colleagues where you currently work. In other cases, people may be expecting a job change for you because of changes or downsizing within a department. Whether your departure is comfortable or unexpected and awkward, you want to leave with as much grace and goodwill as possible.

Consider the following tips as you plan your exit from your present employer:

■ **Be firm in your decision to leave. Do not waiver.** One of the benefits of giving yourself time before you accept or negotiate a job offer is that you avoid having second thoughts after you make your decision. Carefully consider the pros and cons of staying or accepting a new position. Be sure that you really want to leave your present position. Don't use a job offer as a test of your present employer's commitment to you.

■ **Don't consider a counteroffer from your present employer.** When you tell your present employer that you have been offered another job, don't do so with the hope that they will make a counteroffer. (A counteroffer, or *buyback,* is the strategy of offering you a raise to keep you from leaving.)

Research shows that most people who accept a counteroffer do not stay with the company for a long time. Basically, the buyback gives the company enough time to find a replacement for you; then you'll be out of a job or forced to accept something less attractive within the company.

■ **Leave on good terms.** Don't use your letter of resignation as the opportunity to say all the negative things you've wanted to say to your bosses or irritating employees. Always try to maintain positive relationships within the company, because situations change and your networks are important for reasons you can't always anticipate.

Sample letter of resignation

Even though you may be eager to begin your new job as quickly as possible, you owe your present employer a reasonable amount of time for the company to adjust to your absence and/or train a replacement. You should express your willingness to participate in training or transitioning a replacement within a reasonable timeframe. Your letter should also express appreciation for your work experience there and express wishes for the company's continued success.

When you come to the point of submitting a letter of resignation, consider the following model. People usually hand-deliver this type of letter. If you work in a different geographic location than your supervisor, then you can mail it. In that case, include your name, your address, and the date, just as you would any other letter you mail.

Date

Dear Susan:

I am writing to inform you that I have taken a position as Manager of Operations with XZY Company and expect to start there on the first of September.

Working with you has been a pleasure and a real opportunity to learn and grow in management skills. You have taught me much, and I am indeed grateful.

If I can be helpful in training my replacement or in facilitating a transition, please count on my full support.

Again, let me thank you for all your support and encouragement in the past. I wish you continued success, and I look forward to staying in touch.

Sincerely,

Your name

In your letter of resignation, give adequate notice, offer to assist in the transition, and express appreciation for the people and job you are leaving.

Networking Follow-up

A successful job search is usually the result of your own skills and hard work, plus the support and guidance of your professional network. Just as you want to celebrate completing a winning job-interview process, you want to share the good news with your network so that they can feel good about the roles they played in this process.

Making phone calls

Right after you accept your new job, sit down and make a list of all the people who helped you with the interview process and your job search. This list identifies your network, or group of colleagues, mentors, and associates who have supported and encouraged you. You don't want to lose track of these people, and you do want to express gratitude for their efforts on your behalf.

Use the form in Table 11-2 to keep track of the people who have assisted you in the interviewing process.

Table 11-2 Networking Checklist

Name	Contact Information	Date	Type of Contact

You can develop a code for Type of Contact — perhaps a T to represent a telephone call, E for e-mail, N for thank-you note, and L for letter.

Contact the people closest to your job search by phone to share your good news. When you make the phone call, indicate that you have good news to share and thank the person for a specific contribution he or she made to the process. Express your interest in continuing to stay in touch and suggest a time for a follow-up call or lunch after you've settled into your new job.

After you suggest a time to call or get together, insert this event into your calendar or computer to remind you to get back in touch at the appropriate time.

Sending your thank-yous

You should send everyone who helped you in your job-search process thank-you notes or letters — including the people you've already phoned. This courtesy goes a long way in continuing the positive energy and goodwill that helped motivate you during the interviewing process.

Like every good thank-you note, this one should be personal, warm, and specific. Don't send a form letter! The people in your professional network will want to stay onboard and continue to mentor your development and growth if they think that they've made a positive contribution to your professional growth. Let them know how much you appreciate what they've done and express your hopes for the future.

Congratulations! You've successfully conducted your winning job-interview process. The lessons you learned in this process — being prepared, doing your research, staying organized, and expressing gratitude — will transfer to your new situation. Good luck.

CLIFFSNOTES REVIEW

Use this CliffsNotes Review to practice what you've learned in this book and to build your confidence in your interviewing skills. After you work through the review questions, the problem-solving exercises, and the fun and useful practice projects, you're well on your way to achieving your goal of using your interviewing skills to obtain the job you desire.

Q&A

1. Making a good impression on the interviewer starts with
   a. negotiating a compensation package
   b. scheduling the interview
   c. dressing for a successful interview
   d. researching job opportunities on the Internet

2. A good way to learn about the company you are interviewing with is
   a. talking with employees who work there
   b. reading their annual report
   c. researching on the Internet
   d. all of the above

3. Interviewers usually ask questions about
   a. strengths and weaknesses
   b. family and friends
   c. vacation benefits
   d. competitive products

4. The best way to reduce anxiety before an interview is to
   a. buy expensive clothes for the interview
   b. research, prepare, and practice for the interview
   c. arrive just on time
   d. all of the above

5. Your answers to the interview questions involve both

   a. preparation and phone calls

   b. honesty and letters

   c. verbal and non-verbal communication

   d. all of the above

6. If you are asked an inappropriate question in an interview, you should

   a. call the police

   b. ask for an interpreter

   c. answer it briefly

   d. avoid answering directly

7. When the interview is over, you should

   a. express your interest in the job and in the company

   b. rush to catch your cab

   c. indicate that you will be too busy to be reached next week

   d. all of the above

8. To increase your chances of a second interview

   a. make a follow-up phone call

   b. ask your network for suggestions

   c. alert your references that they might be contacted

   d. all of the above

9. To negotiate a better compensation package

   a. bring up the issue of salary in the first interview

   b. ask how many vacation days you will get

   c. research what industry standards for salary are

   d. all of the above

10. To conclude a successful job interview, you should

   a. get to work right away

   b. prepare letters of acceptance and resignation

   c. go on vacation

   d. all of the above

Answers: 1. b; 2. d; 3. a; 4. b; 5. c; 6. d; 7. a; 8. d; 9. c; 10. b

Scenario

1. How would you answer the interview question, "I notice a gap in your employment history. What have you been doing?"

   a. You are going on an interview after a prolonged absence from the corporate workplace because of an unsuccessful small business venture.

   b. You have been unemployed for over a year after being laid off or fired from a previous job.

   c. You have taken time off from the corporate world to raise a family and your training and skills are now out-of-date.

Consider This

■ Did you know that you can turn even negative employment experiences like getting fired into a positive interview impression? See Chapters 3 and 7.

■ Did you know that your network of professional colleagues can be a great asset in developing winning interviewing skills? See Chapters 5 and 11.

■ Did you know that listening skills are at least as important as preparing good answers to tough questions? See Chapter 6.

Practice Projects

1. Getting a Job Interview from a Classified Ad.

Take a look at the classified ad section of your local newspaper. Select one ad that seems related to your job search and write a cover letter that you think would get the attention of the interviewer and help you schedule an interview.

2. Getting a Job Interview at a Job Fair

Imagine that you have a 15-minute opportunity to talk with an interviewer at a local job fair. Prepare a written response to the questions about experience, strengths, and career goals. Practice selling your skills with another friend for a 15-minute time segment.

CLIFFSNOTES RESOURCE CENTER

The learning doesn't need to stop here. CliffsNotes Resource Center shows you the best of the best — links to the best information in print and online about job interviewing skills. And don't think that this is all we've prepared for you; we've put all kinds of pertinent information at www.cliffs-notes.com. Look for these terrific resources at your favorite bookstore or local library and on the Internet. When you're online, make your first stop www.cliffsnotes.com, where you'll find more incredibly useful information about job interviews.

Books

This CliffsNotes book is one of many great books about job interviews published by IDG Books Worldwide, Inc. So if you want some great next-step books, check out these other publications:

Kennedy, Joyce Lain, **Job Interviews For Dummies,** IDG Books, 1996, $12.99.

This book covers just about everything you need to know about interviewing in a fun, easy-to-read way.

Bloch, Ph.D., Deborah Perlmutter, **Have a Winning Job Interview,** NTC LearningWorks, 1992, $12.95.

This book provides answers to the commonly asked interview questions and strategies for dealing with stressful interview situations.

DeLuca, Matthew J., **Best Answers to the 201 Most Frequently Asked Interview Questions,** McGraw-Hill, 1997, $10.95.

This book focuses on possible responses to commonly asked questions about education, experience, work styles, and stress. The book contains practical suggestions for dealing with tough questions.

Drake, John D., **The Perfect Interview: How to Get the Job You Really Want,** 2nd edition, American Management Association, 1997, $17.95.

Contains many practical Skill Building Worksheets to perfect interviewing skills.

Eyler, David R., **Job Interviews That Mean Business,** Random House, 1992, $12.00.

This book provides case studies representative of actual interview situations that help develop strategies for successful interviewing.

Farr, J. Michael, **The Quick Interview & Salary Negotiation Book,** JIST Works, Inc., 1995, $12.95.

Contains quick tips and sites references for further investigation. Summarizes information about salary ranges for specific industries.

Kay, Andrea, **Interview Strategies That Will Get You the Job You Want,** Betterway Books, 1996, $12.99.

Written by a professional career consultant, the author provides quick checklists to help the interviewer develop successful strategies for a winning job interview.

Hirsch, Arlene. **The National Business Employment Weekly Premier Guide to Interviewing (3rd Edition),** Wiley, 1999, $12.95.

Another great interviewing guide.

Finding books published by IDG Books Worldwide Inc. and other publishers is easy. They're in your favorite bookstores (on the Internet and at a store near you). We also have three Web sites that you can use to read about all the books we publish:

■ www.cliffsnotes.com

■ www.dummies.com

■ www.idgbooks.com

Internet

Check out these Web sites for more information about job interviews and more:

Career Paths, www.CareerPath.com — provides over 340,000 job listings, company profiles, and industry information.

Career Resources Center, www.fresno.edu/dept/crc — places its emphasis on students pursuing their first careers and provides useful tips on how to manage behavioral interviews.

Department of Labor, www.safetynet.doleta.gov/interview — provides plenty of interview tips and up-to-date information about jobs and interviewing.

Department of Labor, www.K12doleta.gov/interview.htm — has been developed by the DOL Employment and Training Administration and provides articles and tips and suggests practice activities.

Womenswire, www.women.com — provides special listings and tips for jobs and interviewing for women in a variety of industries.

Next time you're on the Internet, don't forget to drop by www.cliffsnotes.com. We created an online Resource Center that you can use today, tomorrow, and beyond.

Magazines & Other Media

The following sources are useful for your research of company profiles, industry trends, and job listings.

Federal Jobs Digest. This biweekly focuses on opportunities in government employment both civilian and military. Lists openings, salaries, and requirements.

Dun and Bradstreet Million Dollar Directories. Provides company profiles with geographic listings in five volumes.

Standard and Poor's Register of Corporations, Directors and Executives. Provides annual information including names, titles, and addresses of officers in leading corporations.

Send Us Your Favorite Tips

In your quest for learning, have you ever experienced that sublime moment when you figure out a trick that saves time or trouble? Perhaps you realized you were taking ten steps to accomplish something that could have taken two. Or you found a little-known workaround that gets great results. If you've discovered a useful tip that helped you deliver a winning job interview more effectively and you'd like to share it, the CliffsNotes staff would love to hear from you. Go to our Web site at www.cliffsnotes.com and click the Talk to Us button. If we select your tip, we may publish it as part of CliffsNotes Daily, our exciting, free e-mail newsletter. To find out more or to subscribe to a newsletter, go to www.cliffsnotes.com on the Web.

INDEX

A

acceptance, letters of, 103–107
active listening, 58–62
affirmations, 41
age, questions about, 66
annual reports, 19
appearance, physical, 37–38, 43
attention, paying, 58–59

B

benefits, 98–101
body language, 43, 77. *See also* appearance, physical; posture
body weight, 66
books, recommended, 115–116
breath, taking a deep, 40–41
buybacks, 108

C

calendar, job search, 7–8, 15
Chambers of Commerce, 20
children, questions about, 65
CliffsNotes Daily, 3, 118
communication
  active listening and, 58–62
  body language and, 43, 77
  small-talk situations, 48–49
  strategies for beginning an interview, 48–50
  strategies for questions and answers, 50, 52–54, 56–57
companies
  learning about, 16–21
  location of, 15
confidence-building, 35–36, 38–39
counteroffers, 108

D

D-A-R format, 72
Department of Labor, 22
directories, 20, 118
disabled individuals, 66

E

ethnicity, questions about, 64–65
etiquette, 10–11, 13–14
eye contact, 61, 71

F

Fair Employment Practices
  Commission, 64
feedback, 45–46, 57, 62
fired, questions about having been, 68–69

G

goals
  career, questions about, 31
  setting realistic, for interviews, 42–45
gratitude, expressing, 84, 86, 110–111

H

handicapped individuals. *See* disabled individuals
handshakes, 81
health, 66
honesty, 51

I

icons, used in this book, 2
Internet. *See* Web sites
interviews. *See also* communication; questions
  appropriate actions after, 83–85
  beginning of, 48–50
  behavioral, 72
  end of, 75–82
  making phone calls to set up, 8–13
  meal, 90–92
  negotiating skills for, 93–102
  panel, 71
  preparing for, 5–8, 14–15
  questions and answers part of, 29, 50–52, 54–57, 64–65, 67–69, 71
  second, 44–45, 83–87, 89–90, 92
  serial, 89–90
  situational, 73–74

interviews *(continued)*
  skills for, practicing, 24–25, 27, 29–34, 39
  transition to the main part of, 49–50

L

last impressions, 81
letters
  acceptance, 103–107
  resignation, 107–110
  thank-you, 82, 84, 86 –87, 111
listening skills, 8–9, 58–61

M

magazines, recommended, 118
marital status, 65

N

names, of people, 14, 44, 86
negotiating
  benefits, 98–101
  compensation packages, 100
  research for, 94–95
  salaries, 93, 96–101
nervousness
  building confidence to counteract, 35–36, 38–39
  dealing with stage fright, 39–42
networking
  after interviews, 87
  after you accept a new job, 110–111
  basic description of, 21
  learning about companies through, 20–21
  using phone calls for, 12–14
non-verbal communication. *See* communication
notes, taking, 39, 60–61

P

phone calls
  after you accept a new job, 110–111
  alerting interviewers of unexpected delays, 15
  etiquette for, 10–11, 13–14
  follow-up, 84

improving your skills in handling, 8–11
networking through, 12–14
positive attitude, 67, 72, 99
posture, 37, 118
problem-solving, 51, 73, 90

Q

questions. *See also* communication; interviews
  about how others perceive you, 53
  about past achievements, 56
  about previous experience, 52
  about salary expectations, 56, 96–98
  about your strong points, 54–55
  asked by you, during the interview, 57, 77–78
  common, 29–32, 52–54, 56–57
  dealing with difficult, 68–70
  illegal/inappropriate, 64–67
  strategies for handling, 50, 52–54, 56–57

R

race, questions about, 64–65
RAPP approach, 35–36, 38–39
references, 53, 88–89
referrals, 21
religion, questions about, 64–65
research
  confidence-building and, 36
  Internet resources for, 23, 118
  learning about companies, 16–21
  learning about specific industries, 22–23
  preparing for negotiations through, 93–95
resignation, letters of, 107–110
résumés
  bringing extra copies of, to interviews, 39
  keeping extra copies of, near your phone, 9
  review of, in preparation for interviews, 72
  submitting photographs with, requests for, 65
  when to submit, 11
role-playing, 33, 39, 73

S

salaries, 56, 93–101
scenarios, handling difficult, 71–74
sexual harassment, 70
shaking hands, 81
sitting, posture when, 37
small-talk situations, 48–49
smiling, 40, 81
stage fright, 39–42
strengths and weaknesses, describing
  your, 24–25, 27–28
stretching, 41
summaries, verbal, 59–60

T

telephone calls. *See* phone calls
travel time, planning, 15

V

videotaped interviews, for practice,
  33–34
voice mail, 8–9

W

walking, posture when, 37
wardrobe, 6, 37–38
Web sites
  CliffsNotes Web site, 3, 115–116
  Dummies Web site, 116
  IDG Books Worldwide Web site, 116
  researching specific industries through,
    23, 118
  specializing in information about job
    interviews, 117

CliffsNotes™

Your shortcut to success™ for over 40 years

Computers and Software
Confused by computers? Struggling with software? Let *CliffsNotes* get you up to speed on the fundamentals — quickly and easily. Titles include:

Balancing Your Checkbook with Quicken®
Buying Your First PC
Creating a Dynamite PowerPoint® 2000 Presentation
Making Windows® 98 Work for You
Setting up a Windows® 98 Home Network
Upgrading and Repairing Your PC
Using Your First PC
Using Your First iMac™
Writing Your First Computer Program

The Internet
Intrigued by the Internet? Puzzled about life online? Let *CliffsNotes* show you how to get started with e-mail, Web surfing, and more. Titles include:

Buying and Selling on eBay®
Creating Web Pages with HTML
Creating Your First Web Page
Exploring the Internet with Yahoo!®
Finding a Job on the Web
Getting on the Internet
Going Online with AOL®
Shopping Online Safely